The Economic and Financial Crimes Commission in Nigeria

An Appraisal

The Economic and Financial Crimes Commission in Nigeria

An Appraisal

Patrick Edobor Igbinovia

B.Sc.; M.A.; M.Sc.; M.P.A.; Ph.D.; JP

Professor of Criminology and Criminal Justice and
Former Senior Research Advisor (Security and Strategy, SPDC),
Department of Sociology and Anthropology
Faculty of Social Sciences
University of Benin, Benin City

and

Blessing A. Edobor-Igbinovia, *JP*

B.Ed. (Political Science/Education), University of Benin;
M.P.A. (Public Administration), Benson Idahosa University;
Department of Political Science
School of Arts and Social Sciences
College of Education, Ekiadolor, Benin City

Safari Books Ltd
Ibadan

Published by
Safari Books Ltd
Ile Ori Detu
1, Shell Close
Onireke, Ibadan.
Email: safarinigeria@gmail.com

© Patrick Edobor Igbinovia & Blessing A. Edobor-Igbinovia

Publisher: Chief Joop Berkhout, *OON*
Deputy Publisher: George Berkhout

Frist published 2014

ISBN: 978-978-8431-39-8

Dedication

This book is dedicated to the evergreen memories of the special women in our lives, our mothers: Chief (Mrs) Fatimah Oge Igbinovia and Deaconess (Mrs) Alice Onaghise Omokaro, both of blessed memories; Chief Henry Oghogho Ogbodu (SAN) for his steadfast and uncommon friendship and brotherliness; and Professor (Enogie) & Mrs. G.I. Akenzua (OON) for their parental care and unalloyed love.

Acknowledgements

We are immensely grateful to Prof. Eghosa Osagie, former Director of Research, National Institute for Policy and Strategic Studies (NIPPS); and former Vice-Chancellor, Benson Idahosa University, Benin City; Prof. A.A. Akinsanya (Department of Political Science, Tai Solarin University); Professor P.T. Ahire, former Secretary of the Presidential Electoral Reform Committee and Chairman, Benue State Independent Electoral Commission for writing the forewords to this book ; TETFUND, University of Benin and its University Reasearch and Publication Committee for their support.

We are also profoundly grateful to Prof. V.O. Modo, former Dean, Faculty of Social Sciences, University of Uyo for reading and making useful suggestions on the manuscript, Prof. Vincent O. Aghayere (Dean and Professor of Public Administration, Faculty of Management Sciences, Ambrose Alli University, Ekpoma, Edo State) and Nicholas Ogieva (University of Benin) for their immense inputs, invaluable contributions and useful suggestions which have improved the quality of and enhanced the richness of this work. We are highly indebted to them all. May God bless you all.

Preface

This book is a pioneering and pioneer work on a law enforcement agency – the EFCC in Nigeria. The subject of law enforcement is not only fascinating, the academic discourse on the subject is also very compelling.

It is both compelling and interesting partly because it deals with important aspects of the political state institution or agency of social control; with enormous reach and powers with monumental ramifications and consequences for the polity and citizenry. Indeed, as an academic discipline, the science of law enforcement is the study – scientific study – of the role of law enforcement apparatus, agencies, organizations and institutions which are charged with the responsibilities of ensuring that the rules, laws, and regulations of the political state, entity or commonwealth are obeyed and not flouted for the welfare, well-being and common good of the commonwealth.

The subject is also at once compelling, fascinating and interesting because there is a mix of politics in law enforcement and a mix of law enforcement in politics which the authors of this book could not resist exploring in the Nigerian milieu. Our academic training, professional and experiential exposure to the science of law enforcement and political science made this imperative.

For the senior partner or author, for example, such exposure presented itself through education when he obtained first and second degrees specializing in Law Enforcement Administration and Police Science in 1976 (B.Sc) and 1977 (M.A.), respectively. To underscore his unalloyed interest in the subject, he has also written extensively on the subject matter in scholarly and professional outlets, perhaps, more than any other Nigerian academic in the field of Criminology and Criminal Justice Sciences. The first written scholarly essay was on "Police Administration in Modern Nigeria" (*Police Studies:* 1980). Before and after then, his masters and doctorate dissertations were, respectively, on *Police Manpower Selection: A Model for the Nigeria Police Force* (College of Criminology & Criminal Justice, Sam Houston State University, 1977); and *Africa In International Policing: The Development And Operational Dynamics of I.C.P.O – Interpol In Continental Africa* (The School of Criminology and Criminal Justice, The Florida State University, 1983).

The co-authored book titled THE ECONOMIC AND FINANCIAL CRIMES COMMISSION (EFCC) IN NIGERIA: AN APPRAISAL was impelled in pursuant to that specific interest and fascination with law enforcement by the authors.

The EFCC is a very important state institution in Nigeria which was created a decade ago to help stem economic and financial crimes in the country. Of the multitude of law enforcement agencies in the country, the EFCC, in terms of expectation and perception of the Nigerian public, government, international donor agencies and the international community is, perhaps, the most important Nigerian state law enforcement institution.

Unfortunately, despite the prominence or notoriety of the EFCC, there have been few attempts to scientifically appraise the performance of the agency. This is the main problem that this book has attempted to address and redress.

The seminal book consists of 6 chapters which are complemented or supplemented with 13 tables and 10 cartoon depictions on or impressions of EFCC performance.

To realize our goal or aim, this book dealt with the historical background, legal basis and philosophy which lies behind the development of the EFCC; detailing its present set-up, structure, apparatus for carrying out its operational functions and how well it has executed its roles. The book also analyzed the constraints and problems the agency have had to grapple with and how these had impeded its roles; and their ramifications for the agency and polity.

Indeed, the book appraised the functional performance of the agency from its inception in 2003 to 2013; to ascertain if it had been able to meet the aims, missions and visions for its creation. Factors which impacted or vitiated the agency's performance over the period were identified and remedies tendered to help stem them to enable the EFCC enhance their functional performances.

From the scientific appraisal of the performance of the EFCC, the overall conclusion was that the performances of the agency have been halting and mixed, but with overwhelming or preponderance of the evidence weighing clearly to the verdict that the agency has performed less than expected from 2003 to 2013. The net implication of this is that the agency, has, in large measures, been unable to realize its mandates.

Patrick Edobor Igbinovia, Ph.D; JP.
Professor of Criminology & Criminal Justice;
Former Assistant Professor of Criminology and Criminal Justice, Alabama State University, Montgomery, USA;
Former Senior Research Advisor for Security & Strategy (SPDC)
B.Sc. (Criminology and Criminal Justice, 1976: Northwestern Oklahoma State University, Alva, Oklahoma)
M.A. (Criminology and Criminal Justice, 1977: Sam Houston State University, Huntsville, Texas)
M.Sc. (Manpower and Industrial Relations, 1980: University of North Texas, Denton, Texas)
M.P.A. (Public Law/Public Policy, 1982: The Florida State University, Tallahassee, Florida)
Ph.D. (Criminology and Criminal Justice, 1983: The Florida State University, Tallahassee, Florida)

Blessing A. Edobor-Igbinovia, JP
B.Ed. (Political Science/Education, 1992: University of Benin, Benin City)
M.P.A. (Public Administration, 2012: Benson Idahosa University, Benin City)
July 3, 2013

Foreword (I)

Professor Patrick Igbinovia's book, *The Economic and Financial Crimes Commission (EFCC): An Appraisal* is a bold and pioneering effort to professionally evaluate the foremost anti-graft agency in Nigeria.

Since its creation in 2002 and commencement of operation in 2003, the Economic and Financial Crimes Commission (EFCC) has not been subjected to any systematic and scholarly assessment.

Professor Igbinovia has deployed his rich and extraordinary talents in this book to critically examine the historical/philosophical background to the establishment of the EFCC, its legal framework, organizational structure, functions, tools, functional performance, achievements and challenges. Drawing insights from popular literature, consisting mainly of articles in newspapers, magazines, internet etc; coupled with a robust review of the scanty academic literature on this subject, the author has made profound revelations on the functional performance of the EFCC.

It will be recalled that between 1995 and 2003, Nigeria acquired notoriety as the most corrupt country in the world by all standards. The country's domestic and international image was soiled by the wide prevalence of advance fee fraud, money laundering, counterfeiting, illegal charge transfers, futures market fraud, credit card fraud, fraudulent encashment of negotiable instruments, contract scam, etc. The EFCC was created to fight these vices and given enormous powers under its enabling law. This book reveals how the EFCC has fared to date.

By the testimony of successive EFCC Chairmen, the EFCC has achieved remarkable success. They point to the recovery of some ill-gotten assets, criminal conviction of some scammers, sanitization of the banking sector, reduction of oil theft and oil bunkering, on-going arrests and prosecutions, etc, as evidence of success.

However, Prof. Igbinovia's book has shown us that different administrations in Nigeria have used the EFCC for self-preservation and survival. He demonstrates, for instance, how the agency was used under President Olusegun Obasanjo to terrorize political opponents and to exculpate friends, destabilize opposition States, illegally block the candidature of certain political aspirants, etc. All these while ignoring allegations against Obasanjo himself.

President Umaru Yar' Adua allowed the EFCC to be bulldozed by his Attorney General and Minster of Justice who was accused of defending the corrupt, shirking his duty of prosecuting corrupt public officials, frustrating the anti-graft war, interfering with the agency's work, etc.

Under President Goodluck Jonathan, the EFCC is accused of shielding corrupt public office holders and not being serious with the anti-graft war. The President's grant of pardon to some fugitive offenders is perceived as the last nail in the coffin of the anti-corruption war.

The author has adopted highly innovative research techniques to navigate the anti-research posture of the EFCC and assess its functional performance. His overall verdict: negative or at best mixed performance especially in the mandate functions of the agency. The recommendations made to improve the agency's performance are rich and comprehensive.

I recommend this book to scholars, researchers, lawyers, students, criminal justice practitioners and all those interested in the progress of the anti-graft campaign in the country and beyond.

Philip Terdoo Ahire, Ph.D (Cambridge)
Professor of Criminology
Former Secretary of the Nigerian Presidential Electoral Reform Committee; and
Chairman, Benue State Independent Electoral Commission

September 2, 2013

Foreword (II)

One of Nigeria's efforts to reintegrate herself in the international community where it was regarded as a Pariah during the harrowing days of General Sanni Abacha (1993-1998) as the country returned to civilian rule, some would say 'democratic' rule, was the establishment of institutions to confront frontally the scourge of corruption.

The creation of the ICPC and EFCC heralded a major concern about the depth of corruption in the country's life. Indeed, the imperative of confronting and combating the disease has been underscored by the effects of corruption on societal growth and development. Not only has corruption undermined political institutions by weakening the legitimacy and accountability of governments; it also reduces the effectiveness of so-called aid-funded development projects and weakens public support for overseas development assistance programmes in the donor countries.

Put differently, corruption is inimical to sustainable development, poverty reduction and alleviation and good governance. Essentially, corruption has led to pauperisation, inequalities, crimes of monumental proportions, unemployment, brain drain and insurgency that Nigeria has witnessed in the last three decades since the Shehu Shagari Administration.

When one of Africa's foremost criminologists contacted me to write a Foreword to this book on the Economic and Financial Crimes Commission, one of the agencies established by the Obasanjo Administration (1999 – 2007) to confront frontally the scourge of corruption, I readily agreed.

It is, indeed, a great pleasure for me to read the thoughts of someone that I have come to cherish as a brother and colleague since we crossed each other's path when Patrick Edobor Igbinovia started his career as a University Teacher in Nigeria at the University of Ilorin where I was the Foundation Professor of Political Science in mid-1983 and he was a Senior Lecturer and later Reader in Criminology; and thereafter became an Associate Professor and Professor in Criminology at the University of Benin, Benin City.

After reading what Patrick and co-author have to say about the much-dreaded EFCC which later turned out to be used by the powers to be to whip some "opponents" into line, I can not but marvel at the analytical minds of the authors, namely, how they are able, with much elegance, to distill facts from fiction about the role of the EFCC in Nigeria's political economy.

The presentation has been very organised and lucid. One does not need nor require An Advanced Learners Dictionary to be able to understand what the authors are saying and/or have tried to tell the reading public. My only concern, however, is the EFCC has lost the steam and focus under the Jonathan Administration.

It is, therefore, my pleasure to recommend to anyone including budding scholars who are interested in knowing much about the Economic and Financial Crimes Commission. I so recommend this book without any reservations whatsoever.

Adeoye A. Akinsanya
Professor of Political Science
B.Sc. (Political Science), Ibadan; M.P.A. (Pittsburg); M.A., PhD. (Political Science) (Chicago)
Tai Solarin University of Education,
Ijagun,Via Ijebu-Ode,
Ogun State, Nigeria.

August 21, 2013.

Foreword (III)

Until the early years of the twenty-first century, Nigerian Government did not take seriously the problem of corruption. Military Governments during the 1960s, 1970s and 1980s took widely publicized decisions to address this hydra-headed monster which were decisively draconian in the treatment of public officials accused of corruptly enriching themselves.

Yet, and indeed ironically, the period of military rule and the succeeding Fourth Republic are likely to go down in history as one in which the country attained the zenith of corruption.

The question that readily comes to mind is: what are the reasons for this intriguing disconnect between rigorous treatment of corruption and the continuously deteriorating standards of transparency and accountability in Nigeria?

There is an important relationship between economic reform and corruption which is very often ignored. Specifically, corruption creates the conditions which make calls for economic reform strident. Unfortunately, aspects of reform packaged as structural adjustment programmes create ample opportunities for more serious manifestations of corruption without correcting the conditions that promote economic decline.

I will be more specific here. In the early 1980s, a period that may be considered the origin of the current (2013) economic problems, the Federal Government wisely sought advice on how to handle the then emerging challenges of budget deficits, external deficits, inflation and unemployment. An option then was to address, in a serious manner, the issue of financial indiscipline being exhibited by the political class while totally dismissing the option of devaluation of the Naira.

Addressing the problem of corruption in 1982, which then took the form of contact over-invoicing, foreign exchange round-tripping, under-invoicing of exports and over-invoicing of imports would have comprehensively resolved the economic problems identified above. It could have been likened to a malaria patient taking relatively cheap prescribed medication leading to quick recovery. Alternatively, the evaluation option favoured since September 1986 can be likened to a doctor subjecting a malaria patient to a major surgical operation while completely ignoring the malaria problem.

The late recognition of corruption by the major donor agencies and the international financial institutions (World Bank and IMF) as a major driver of economic under-performance paved the way for the establishment of anti-graft agencies in Nigeria. It was generally expected that the Economic and Financial Crimes Commission (EFCC) would stem the tide of corruption in Nigeria.

It is, therefore, appropriate that this well-researched and documented publication appears one full decade after the establishment of the EFCC.

This book attempts to assess the performance of the EFCC in the first ten years of its existence. It employs different scientific statistical techniques (mainly descriptive statistics) to carry out this delicate assignment. Inspite of obvious difficulties encountered in the collection of statistics, it succeeds in arriving at conclusions and making recommendations which are important for the future.

The analysis carried out in the book suggests a number of critical questions that should be wisely and honestly answered. Specifically:

- Was the EFCC established to fight corruption, persecute perceived political enemies or satisfy the requirements of donor agencies?

- Do we really expect the EFCC to seriously address the problem of corruption when its leadership is under the strict control of the President and the Attorney-General?

- Do we not run into the phenomenon of diminishing returns when, in addition to the EFCC, a multiplicity of other official agencies are involved in the same assignment?

- Is the fight against corruption consistent with a national political system distinguished by money politics, largely unregulated free market economy, immunity of key political leaders to judicial prosecution for economic crimes committed during their tenure in office (a strange "privilege" granted by the corruption-friendly 1999 Constitutions)?

Nigeria needs to make progress in her fight against formidably entrenched corruption. Failure in this struggle ensures that the Nigerian economy will remain permanently underdeveloped, render the struggle against violent crime and insurgency an uphill assignment, and most important, compromise political stability.

Professor Eghosa Osagie
B.A. (Economics): Claremont College, California
M.A. (Economics): University of California, Berkeley, California
Ph.D. (Economics): University of California, Los Angeles, California
Former Vice Chancellor, Benson Idahosa University, Benin City, Nigeria; and
Former Director of Research and Studies, National Institute for Policy and Strategic Studies (NIPPS), Kuru, Nigeria.

August 23, 2013

Table of Contents

Page

Dedication v

Acknowledgements vii

Preface ix

Foreword (I) xiii

Foreword (II) xvii

Foreword (III) xix

Table of Contents xxiii

List of Tables xxvii

List of Cartoons xxix

Chapter 1: Introduction

Introduction 1

Chapter 2: Literature Review

Review of the Literature 5

Definition and Purpose 5

Review of the Popular Literature 8

Review of the Academic Legal Literature 13

Review of the Related Literature 15

Chapter 3: Research Methodology

Research Methodology 21

Background to the Research Setting 21

Source and Method of Data Collection 23

Method of Data Analysis 26

Rationale, Benefits and Challenges 27

Chapter 4: Historical Background, Legal Status and Organizational Structure of the EFCC

Background to the Discourse 33

History and Rationale for the Establishment
    of the EFCC 40

Legal Status and Organizational Structure
    of the EFCC 45

Chapter 5: Appraisal of the Performance of the EFCC in Multiple Contexts

Introduction... 61

The Performance of the EFCC as seen in the
    EFCC Context 62

The Performance of the EFCC under
    President Olusegun Obasanjo 71

The Performance of the EFCC under
    President Umaru Yar'Adua 74

The Performance of the EFCC under
President Goodluck Jonathan 76

The Performance of the EFCC as seen in the
    Public Context 85

The Performance of the EFCC as seen from
    Variegated Contexts 4

The Enabling Act and EFCC Performance 108

Plea Bargaining and EFCC Performance 117

The Electoral Process and EFCC Role Performance 131

The Performance of the EFCC as seen from the

    Research Context 134

The Performance of the EFCC as seen in a

    Conclusive Context 146

Chapter 6: Summary, Findings, Conclusions and Recommendations

Summary 153

Findings.. 154

Conclusion.. 157

Recommendations 163

Appendices 173

Bibliography 187

Index 207

List of Tables

TABLE 1:   Transparency International's Ten Most Corrupt Nations in the World 2002   37

TABLE 2:   Transparency International's Most Corrupt Nations in the World (1999 – 2003)   37

TABLE 3:   Bank Fraud in Nigeria from 1989 to 1999   38

TABLE 4:   Forgery and Fraud Cases in Nigerian Banks (2000–2001)   39

TABLE 5:   Amount of Money Allegedly Misappropriated in Federal Government Ministries (2001)   40

TABLE 6:   Record of EFCC Related Investigations and Convictions (2003 – 2011)   68

TABLE 7:   Record of EFCC Recoveries from June 2008 to March 2011   69

TABLE 8:   Politically Exposed Persons (PEPs) Standing Trial Who Contested During 2007 and 2011 Polls   70

TABLE 9:   Countries Surveyed in the 2010 Global Integrity Report   86

TABLE 10:   Ethno-Religious Domination of Top
            and Strategic Positions in the EFCC
            as at November 22, 2011   104

TABLE 11:   Record Average Performance of EFCC
            and ICPC (2005);   137

TABLE 12:   Functional Performance Appraisal
            Scorecard of EFCC Based on
            Literature Findings   140

TABLE 13:   Functional Performance Appraisal
            Scorecard Rating of EFCC Based on
            Enabling Act Mandate – Specific
            Functions and Literature Findings   141

List of Cartoons

Cartoon A: Who Will Dare The President?   91

Cartoon B: Corruption and EFCC Chairman's
Tenure Elongation   97

Cartoon C: The Plea Bargain;   118

Cartoon D: Again, The Plea Bargain   120

Cartoon E: Yet Again, The Plea Bargain   120

Cartoon F: Nigeria's Application of Plea Bargain
Decries   121

Cartoon G: The Notorious Armed Robber and Plea
Bargain   121

Cartoon H: EFCC As A Bloody Toothless Dog!   147

Cartoon I: EFCC Before and Now   148

Cartoon J: EFCC Blunted by Corruption   148

Chapter 1

Introduction

There are many law enforcement or security agencies created by government in Nigeria to meet certain and specific situations or purposes or to deal with various issues and problems of concern to government or on matters bothering on specific law enforcement and security issues. Some of these agencies are: the Nigeria Police Force; the State Security Service; National Intelligence Agency; Defence Intelligence Agency; National Drug Law Enforcement Agency; National Copyright Commission; Code of Conduct Commission; National Agency For Food and Drug Administration and Control; Independent Corrupt Practices Commission; and the Economic and Financial Crimes Commission, among others.

As can be deduced or even inferred from their individual names, titles or nomenclatures, each agency has its area of jurisdiction or focus; and each agency is a creation of government by Statute, Acts or Laws or Constitution. For example, the main mission of the Independent Corrupt Practices Commission (ICPC) and the Economic and Financial Crimes Commission (EFCC), is to fight or stem corruption and corrupt practices (ICPC); and economic and financial crimes (EFCC), respectively. Note must be made also that both the Nigeria Police Force and the Code of Conduct Commission are creations of the Nigerian

Constitution. The Police even has an enabling act (The Police Act) to regulate it.

Of the numerous law enforcement or security agencies in Nigeria, perhaps, the EFCC is one of the most important in terms of the perception of Nigerian public, government, international donor agencies, and the international community. This statement finds support in the amount of money and material expended on it and the contributions it gets from the aforementioned bodies.

It is for this reason that this important organization captivates the attention of all and sundry and has gingered the need to study it. It behoves us to, therefore, take a studied and scientific appraisal, evaluation, assessment and scrutiny of its critical role and how it has met that role in Nigeria bearing in mind that the EFCC is a very important state institution.

The EFCC was created in 2002 as an anti-graft agency. It officially began its operations on April 16, 2003. From the year 2003 to 2013, the agency has been functioning for about ten years. The EFCC, therefore, offers interesting research possibilities because it is still in a very active stage of transition and development. This process of change is important for the study of the administration of justice. To be able to document the changing and developmental concepts of the EFCC in Nigeria would, therefore, be of inestimable value.

Unfortunately, there have been few attempts to explore or appraise the performance of the agency scientifically or to document the activities of such an important arm of state. Indeed, the subject has been long neglected in the scientific literature. This is a major problem this book attempted to address and redress.

In this book, we discuss the historical background, legal basis and philosophy which lie behind the development of the

EFCC. It also explored in detail the present set-up and structure of the agency, its apparatus or tools for executing its operational functions, how well it executed its roles, and analyzed its constraints or problems it grappled with and how they may have impeded its roles and their ramifications for the organization and the polity.

Indeed, the book appraised the functional performance of the agency from the inception till date and ascertained if it had been able to meet the aims, mission and visions for its creation. Factors which have impacted or vitiated its performance over the period were identified and remedies tendered to help stem them to enable it to enhance the functional performance of the organization.

It is hoped, perhaps, that this book contributed to knowledge in this important area of government, facilitated the realization of its goals in the polity, enhanced its overall functionality and helped to enable the agency fulfil its onerous roles and responsibilities to the Nigerian society.

In many ways, therefore, this book hopefully, perhaps, represents a pioneer effort both in its direction and focus. A perusal of the available relevant literature, few as it appears, revealed that no systematic analysis of its kind, perhaps, has ever been attempted or undertaken on the EFCC. This was a major motivation for this book.

As was highlighted earlier, the EFCC was created in 2002 as a specialized law enforcement agency to fight and help stem the pervasive economic and financial crimes in Nigeria. Indeed, the need to launder the battered image of the country and Nigerians basically informed the establishment of the ICPC (2000) and the EFCC (2002). The activities of the organization, the EFCC, cover the whole of the Nigerian socio-economic landscape. Its powers extend also to all matters involving economic and financial crimes and other related practices in the Nigerian clime. The scope of this book, therefore, covered the operation of the EFCC in the entire Nigerian territory and the legal and jurisdictional confines which the law setting up the agency limits it to. The book marginally also touched on activities of the EFCC which fall incidentally outside the landscape of Nigeria. Indeed, the book area was limited to the operation of the agency in Nigeria mainly and to a lesser extent on its operations outside the shores of Nigeria. Therefore, the study period is between 2003 to 2013.

Chapter 2

Review of Relevant Literature

Definition and purpose

The task of writing a literature review in a research study is an important one. It affords the researcher the opportunity to show how the researchers' work relates to others. It helps the researcher to decide whose work he or she wants to write about, whose work the researcher probably has to write about and how he or she will represent the field as a whole in a general overview.

There are many different definitions and purposes of a literature review. However, the following writers suggest that a review is an interpretation, a synthesis, a project, a task and a new *"look"* at new sources:

> An interpretation and synthesis of published research.
> (Merriam, 1988:6)

> A research project in its own right.
> (Bruce, 1994; Brent, 1986:137)

> A task that continues throughout the duration of the thesis... shows how the problem under investigation relates to previous research.
> (Anderson *et al*, 1970:17)

> [An opportunity to] look again at the literature...in...an
> area not necessarily identical with, but collateral to, your
> own area of study.
>
> (Leedy, 1989:66)

Merriam's use of *'interpretation'* and *'synthesis'* makes clear the active role of the writer; it is the thesis writers' version of the literature, their selection and arrangement of their summaries and critiques. Brent rightly clarifies the research that is required for a review. Anderson, Durston and Poole (1970) emphasize that reviewing the literature is a constant, running through the whole book. Leedy seems to suggest broadening the review's scope.

The review has a *'purpose'* in two senses: on one level the purpose is for the writer to learn about the literature in the course of writing about it, and on another level the review has its own *'purpose'* in that it plays a role in the thesis argument. Both purposes are captured by Bruce:

> Literature reviews in the context of postgraduate study
> may be defined in terms of process and product. The
> process involves the researcher in exploring the literature
> to establish the status quo, formulate a problem or
> research enquiry, to defend the value of pursuing the line
> of enquiry established, and to compare the findings and
> ideas of others with his or her own. The product involves
> the synthesis of the work of others in a form which
> demonstrates the accomplishment of the exploratory
> process.
>
> (Bruce 1994:218)

The rationale for writing the literature review consists of the following:

(a) to establish the status quo;

(b) to formulate a problem;

(c) to defend the value of pursuing the line of enquiry;

(d) to compare the findings and ideas of others' with ones own;

(e) to synthesize the work of others; and

(f) to demonstrate the accomplishment of the exploratory process.

A helpful distinction between the review and the rest of the thesis is provided by Cooper:

> First, a literature review uses as its database reports of primary or original scholarship, and does not report new primary scholarship itself... Second, a literature review seeks to summarise, evaluate, clarify and/or integrate the content of primary reports.
> (Cooper 1988:107)

While Bruce simplifies:

> Typically, the literature review forms an important chapter in the thesis, where its purpose is to provide the background to and justification for the research undertaken.
> (Bruce 1994:218)

For the researcher, reviewing the literature can be a means of learning from others' thought processes, expanding their view of the field, becoming familiar with different theoretical perspectives and parallel developments. Literature review can demonstrate ones ability as a researcher:

Demonstrate that you [have] a professional command of the background theory.
(Phillips and Pugh 2000:59)

The review of literature involves locating, reading and evaluating reports of research as well as reports of casual observation and opinion that are related to... the planned project. It is aimed at obtaining a detailed knowledge of the topic studied.
(Borg and Gall 1989:114)

This is just one of the structures one has to create in a book: an account of the work that has gone before. Who has worked in ones area? Who think ones' subject is important? How does ones work relate to theirs? The rhetorical purpose of the literature review section is to show the *"gap"*, to show that there is a need for ones work.

In this study, the researcher adopted the definitions of the concept as advanced by Merriam, Anderson, et al, and Leedy and, especially, that of Borg and Gall; and viewed the purpose of a literature as encompassing the following elements:

- to give an overview of the 'big issues';
- to select some of these for your study;
- to summarize other people's work;
- to evaluate other people's work;
- to provide a context for your work;
- to identify gaps;
- to develop an understanding of theory and method.

As noted above, the opinion of Borg and Gall (1989:14) were of inestimable value to this researcher in delimiting the confines of the review of the related literature utilized in the study.

Review of the popular literature

The EFCC (Establishment) Act was enacted in 2002 by the National Assembly and amended in 2004. The instruments establishing the EFCC and the organization's handbook indicate that the agency was created to bring sanity to the sordid economic and financial crimes situation in Nigeria.

The EFCC, for all practical purposes, has existed in Nigeria for close to ten years. What is certain, perhaps, is that there is a paucity of scholarly publications or written works about the agency. While we explored this issue later in detail, note must be made here, however, that three main strands of literature were identified concerning the EFCC. These are: The Popular Literature; The Academic Legal Literature; and The Related Academic Literature.

The popular literature consists of essays or opinion pieces, commentaries, editorials in newspapers and electronic media, magazines, internet and other online/ media outlets. They are opinion or news essays which are essentially non-academic or non-scholarly but which nonetheless report on the activities of the EFCC from time to time from the point of view of the public, the writers, EFCC officials and sundry individuals. In general, they carry news items/commentaries about all activities that the agency may be involved in just as they feature news and commentaries on general happenings around the world.

This type of popular outlets has some distinguishing features: they are basically news items, opinion pieces, commentaries; they reflect what is happening that is regarded

9

as news-worthy to the public; are generally not scholarly in the scientific or academic sense; they are often very sensational, non-scientific and carry exaggerated and loud headlines which may not truly hide their bias or slant. Nevertheless, these outlets pervade the Nigerian clime yet they play a critical function: they report on EFCC activities as they are seen, watts and all, and help to gauge how the agency and its work are perceived by the public and other commentators. These types of write-ups on the EFCC are numerous but flawed to some extent in terms of scholarly expectations and standards. However, they are not in the least useless but are useful in complementing other sources of information to enable the researcher have a holistic view of the agency and its activities.

The contextual relevance, currency, usefulness and indispensability of this type of literature cannot be overemphasized. How invaluable it is can be demonstrated by the fact that it helps to monitor and report what is happening in the country, and how the public and other commentators and stakeholders think about the agency, view their activities and indicate the direction the agency may be going.

Consequently, these raw data sources, despite some perceived weaknesses and flaws, were invaluable to the realization of the objectives of this research. Indeed, the importance and germaneness of this source of data can be gleaned from the various issues and subjects covered which pertain, generally to the EFCC, and more specifically, to the research topic as exemplified below by the following sample magazine and newspaper publications and articles:

- "The New Anti-Crime Czar" (2003). *THISDAY*, August 30:45.

- "Audu Sue EFCC For Declaring Him Wanted" (2006). *Vanguard*, October 10:1, 14.

- "EFCC: Between Petition, Conviction" (2006). *Vanguard*. October 10:18.

- "EFCC Liaises With INEC Against Corrupt Governors, Others" (2006). *Vanguard*. December: 10.

- "No Gov Cleared Yet – EFCC" (2006). *Vanguard*. October 10:1, 15.

- "EFCC Arrest Ex-Kogi Governor" (2006). *The Punch*. November 30:9.

- "Dariye: The Final Rush" (2006). *Tell*: 27.

- "EFCC's Last Act" (2007). *Vanguard*. February 22:31.

- "EFCC, It is the Return of the Nigeria Police" (2007) *Vanguard*. February: 18.

- "Governors on Their Knees" (2007). *Tell*, No. 22 May 28: 20.

- "EFCC Now To Concentrate On Money Laundering, Terrorism" (2007). *Vanguard*. July 2:1, 15.

- "EFCC Minus Ribadu" (2007). *Vanguard*. July 19:31.

- "EFCC Arrests Kalu, Turaki" (2007). *Vanguard*. July 12:1, 15.

- "Graft: No Protection For My Sponsors – Yar'Adua" (2007). *Vanguard*. August 7:1, 15.

- "Controversial Directive On EFCC" (2007). *Vanguard*. August 12:10.

- "Ex-Governors are Scapegoats" (2007). *Vanguard*. August 12:10.

- "How Yar'Adua Reversed Self On EFCC, ICPC, Conduct Tribunal – Presidency" (2007) *Vanguard*. August 12:11.

- "EFCC Disagrees With Bola Ajibola On Plea Bargain" (2007). *Vanguard*. August 9:1, 15.
- "AG vs EFCC: Aondoakaa's Move has Political Undertone – NBA, WABA, Others" (2007). *Vanguard*. September 21:43 – 46.
- "Aondoakaa: The AGF on the Firing Line" (2007). *Vanguard*. September 21:42.
- "Justice Minister, Aondoakaa, Divides Nigerians, As Confusion Ravages War On Corruption" (2007). *Vanguard*. September 21:19.
- "Ibori: EFCC Adds More Charges" (2007). *Vanguard*. December, 19:10.
- "Ribadu's Course" (2008). *The Nation*. January 7:13.
- "Igbinedion Returns, Faces EFCC today as UN body writes Yar'Adua on Ribadu" (2008). *Vanguard*. January 21:1, 5.
- "Yar'Adua Ends Anti-Corruption War" (2008). *Tell*. No. 2, January.
- "Undertaker Takes Over EFCC: Rest In Piece!" (2008). *Tell*. June 2.
- "Why EFCC is in a Comma" (2008). *Tell*. 48 December 1.
- "EFCC Unserious With Ex-Governor's Trial" (2008). *The Punch*. December 10:1-2.
- "Ribadu's Dismissal: A Blow Against Hope" (2009). *Tell*. January 12:20.
- "A Case of Hunting the Hunter" (2010). *THISDAY*. March 23:25.
- "Waziri Wants Tough Measures to Fight Corruption" (2011). *The Nation*. May 6:6.
- "Orji Kalu: Challenges Before President Jonathan" (2011). *Saturday Sun*. May 7:71.

- "What Nigerians Expect From Jonathan" (2011). *Sunday Sun.* May 8:64.
- "EFCC, Please Walk the Talk" (2011). *The Nation.* May 23:21.
- "Persecution of Ex-Bank Directors" (2011). *Daily Sun.* May 23:20.
- "Akingbola Urges Court to Stop EFCC From Arraigning Him" (2011). *The Nation.* May 24:3.
- "EFCC and Corrupt Politicians" (2011). *Daily Sun.* May 24:18.

Arising from the above, therefore, in the main, from 2003 to 2013, a total of over one hundred and twenty contextually-relevant, project-germane and topic-related published articles, opinion pieces and source materials published in various newsprint outlets, newsmagazines, newspapers and media platforms and reports on the EFCC were identified by the researcher. These sources were consulted, analyzed and scrutinized by these researchers to provide an in-depth and holistic appraisal of the performance of the EFCC in Nigeria.

Equally invaluable and in combination with other data sources to the realization of the objectives of this research were internet sources. As indicated in the methodological section of this book, internet surfing yielded over 100 documents that were consulted and analyzed to facilitate the achievement of the end-goals of this book.

Review of academic legal literature

It is at once a paradox and also an astonishing phenomenon that while the EFCC is a household name in Nigeria and its activities are reported and receive wide mention almost on a daily basis in the popular literature, it is astonishing that that popularity, or as some would probably say, notoriety, has not been matched by scholarly efforts, academic treatise, or scientific write-ups or study about the agency or organization in the standard journals and outlets.

Even the few scholarly essays currently available are too generic to be germane or meaningful contextually. They are conspicuously noted for focusing and dealing exclusively with issues that are tangential to the EFCC. They focus on topics that have no direct bearing with the subject of this research or the EFCC as an organization. Thus, for example, Vukor-Quarshie (1996) wrote on the development of the criminal law of Nigeria as it relates to economic and financial crimes. Similarly, Ladan (2007) analysed the effectiveness of legal and enforcement framework in fighting advance fee fraud and money laundering activities in Nigeria. Furthermore, Akhikhero (2007) examined the legal dynamics for the enforcement of economic crimes in Nigeria. Similarly, Ocheje (2001) discussed law and social change as they relate to Nigeria's corrupt practices and other related offences using the Act of 2000 as a focal point.

Like the above other articles before it, the essay by Imam and Mustapha (undated) dealt exclusively with the examination of the role of the legislature in combating corruption in Nigeria offering just a brief and passing mention of the EFCC Act.

Arguing basically along the same line, Oyewo (undated) also examined the corruption phenomenon in Nigeria detailing the "governance issues", constitutional mechanisms and framework designed to tackle the phenomenon. He, like, Imam and Mustapha, did not mention any iota of the role of the EFCC in tackling the phenomenon.

On the other hand, Ajagun (2009) was concerned with the evaluation of some selected anti-corruption policies in Nigeria as they relate basically to Edo State. In a few statements, he peripherally touched on the establishment, composition, operations, functions and responsibilities of the EFCC in his 354-page treatise without offering any analysis of the performance or appraisal of the activities of the EFCC or even offering any citation on any scholarly work written on the agency.

The unique features of the above academic legal literature that can be readily identified are: (a) they are legal academic essays which sometimes predated the creation of the EFCC; (b) they are definitely not related to the discussion of the performance of the EFCC as an organization; (c) they are generally written by lawyers and are logically, legalistic in bent; (d) they focus on law and legislation affecting economic and financial crimes and the analysis of same; (e) they point to the fact, and indeed confirm, the paucity of the scientific literature on the EFCC and buttresses the need to address and redress that dearth; (f) they justify the pressing need for this research to fill the void or gap in the scientific discourse of the EFCC.

Review of the related academic literature

There is a need to restate and reiterate a few things here to enhance our understanding of the task at hand.

The scientific, scholarly and academic essays reviewed here are those write-ups which meet standards expected in learning in academic circles. The peer-reviewed write-ups in these last two categories are articles in books, academic journals, magazines, conference and seminar pieces, informed commentaries dealing with the EFCC. These categories are generally more acceptable in the academic domain but, unfortunately, as we have seen, partly due to the inaccessibility of potential researchers/writers to EFCC materials or the uncooperative attitude of EFCC officials in research-related matters or even out of fear or intimation, as alluded to elsewhere in this work, are conspicuously marked by and for their dearth or paucity or scantiness.

Indeed, after close to 10 years of the formal existence of the EFCC, it has found few scientific research efforts directed mainly to its activities. More telling and profound, perhaps, is that there is virtually almost no scientific literature which deals exclusively with the appraisal or assessment of the performance of such an important institution of state.

The closest essays to the topic that one could lay hands on are those of the EFCC (2004), Bello-Imam (2005), Salami (2007), Ribadu (2006, 2009), Enweremadu (2010) and Waziri (2011a and b). The last seven essays are somehow more scientific than the first write-up.

The EFCC *Information Handbook* (2004) provides sketchy information on the functions, powers and structure of the agency. It also discussed the role of the Nigerian Financial Intelligence; and the powers of the courts under the Act setting up the EFCC.

The essay by Bello-Imam titled "The Economic and Financial Crimes Commission (EFCC) in Nigeria", as the topic even suggests, is essentially a description of the various facets of the agency "in its embryonic years of existence" placing emphasis on the establishment, structure and operational basis of the organization. The essay rudimentarily, barely and sketchily touched on the main problems facing the agency and the ways to stem them (Bello-Imam, 2009:219-233).

16

In an article titled "EFCC: Between Perception and Reality" (2006), Nuhu Ribadu, the pioneer Chairman of the EFCC, took a critical stock of the agency from its origin till 2006. He opines that before the EFCC was established, Nigeria was not only corruption-ridden but a pariah nation in the comity of nations. However, in the four years of its (EFCC's) existence (2002 – 2006), he argues, the image of the country changed as the agency took the country to new heights by its successful fight against corruption and graft.

Ribadu's essay (2009) centres briefly on the author's "own modest success" that the agency made during his tenure as Chairman and, specifically, on capital loss and corruption in Nigeria.

In his work titled: "The Economic and Financial Crimes Commission of Nigeria", Salami (2007), employed what he tagged "Political Science Analysis" to attempt to explain and unravel the *modus operandi* of the EFCC. He posits that the EFCC was established as a political instrument to intimidate political opponents of the government of the day by those who initiated and created the agency. He concluded that the EFCC is a political tool of government and government's international partners. Indeed, he concluded, that politics and politics alone determined the creation, operation, activities and actions of the EFCC of Nigeria.

His postulations are, in general, largely exercise in exaggeration. While the essay helped to partially throw some light on the phenomenon he set out to explain, the postulations did not really explain the phenomenon nor did it account for the interplay of forces or variables that affected the role and direction of the EFCC in Nigeria. More fundamentally, perhaps, the author had problems citing one research work that had been done on the EFCC; even none was cited from the popular literature. It is also very obvious that the essay had no direct bearing on the performance of the EFCC as conceived by this researcher in this research work. Indeed, Salami's work is far from being worthless: it helps to promote the research enterprise and charts for us the way forward (Salami, 2007).

In a discussion paper by Enweremadu (2010:1-29) which was published by the Friedrich Ebert Stiftung Foundation, titled Anti-Corruption Policies in Nigeria Under Obasanjo and Yar'Adua: What to do after 2011?, the author takes a critical look at anti-corruption policies under both administrations (Obasanjo and Yar'Adua). He concludes that the success of these policies were not too impressive. He, therefore, recommends a strong priority for anti-corruption policies and a reduction of political interference in the work of the anti-corruption agencies to stem the phenomenon.

On the other hand, Jerryboy (2010) argues in his paper titled "The Role of EFCC in Restoring Nigeria's Past Glory" that the agency has to some extent lived up to its mission of ridding Nigeria off corruption. He came to this conclusion without, however, offering much convincing proofs.

Similarly, in a paper presented in 2011(a) by the former Executive Chairman of the EFCC at the United Nations Conference On Least Development Countries in Istanbul, Turkey, F. Waziri focused on the background of the anti-graft "crusade" in Nigeria, the attendant creation of the EFCC and the reform efforts the agency has put in place to help it meet its mandate and achieve its objectives.

Furthermore, in a paper titled "The Economic And Financial Crimes Commission's (EFCC's) Critical Role in Growing The Economy" which she presented on May 7, 2011(b) to the Nigeria – British Chamber of Commerce, Farida Waziri, the former Chairman of the EFCC, essentially discussed the role she believes the agency had played in growing the Nigerian economy. She presented data which she believes not only buttresses her point but also served to highlight some of the agency's achievements during her tenure. The essay was essentially a rehash of the paper she had earlier presented at the United Nations Conference on Least Developed Countries in Istanbul, Turkey (Waziri, 2011a).

Although the above reviewed essays are germane to the main thrust of this book, they do not directly address the issue of the performance appraisal of the EFCC — our main concern. The effort by Waziri (2011a) is not really identical but is somehow and somewhat collateral to our own area of study.

A methodical, scientific, thorough synthesis of the review of the popular literature, review of the academic legal literature and review of the related academic literature have helped us achieve our research objective of appraising the performance of the EFCC in Nigeria. By interpreting and synthesizing these batteries of literature as advocated, advanced and recommended by Merriam (1988), Bruce (1994), and especially by Borg and Gall (1989), it facilitated the investigation, evaluation, clarification and integration of the planned work; and enhanced our enquiry to accomplish the task in our own area of study.

Chapter 3

Research Methodology

Research methodology is the science of studying how research is to be carried out: It is the procedures or processes by which researchers go about their work of describing, explaining and predicting phenomena. Simply put, research methodology is a systematic way to solve a problem. The heart of any research study is the methodology adopted.

Background to the research setting

A few things can be stated categorically about undertaking research study on the EFCC: it is a tall order getting research information direct from the agency; and the standard or routine or "expected" scientific methods of gathering data (e.g. survey research) would not do or yield any research dividend in the setting.

Conducting survey research on the EFCC is extremely difficult and not easy. The EFCC code even makes it a breach of discipline to reveal any information about the agency to outsiders or to let outsiders of any hue see any documents; and officials of the organization generally are very reluctant to cooperate and are suspicious of any inquiries.

The officials tend to guard information about the agency jealously and carefully. Even the size of the agency is regarded as a secret or confidential information; and the agency officials themselves do not grant access to EFCC documents to the outsiders or researchers and often resist outside observation as an interference in their professional competence, seemingly wondering for what nefarious purposes someone — some busybody/intruder/interloper would want to know about their activities. In sum, one could be in danger inquiring about the agency and its operations. Indeed, one risks possible arrest or being accused of subversion or being charged with the offence of divulging state or official secrets or being in possession of same. On research matters, the government, and particularly, security agencies like the EFCC, are xenophobic: the EFCC is not researcher or research-friendly, as are other Nigerian security organizations. The fear of the EFCC, therefore, is the beginning of wisdom.

Writing to obtain official permission to engage in research concerning their activities amounts to a complete waste of time as correspondences and phone calls are never answered. To even undertake to wait for their response to enquiries would normally consume the better part of any research time set aside.

The researchers, therefore, had to device unique and innovative ways, (see source and method of data collection to rationale, benefits and challenges below) despite some perceived flaws and imperfections, to collect the necessary data or information on the agency. This dilemma is, perhaps, aptly and best summarized by a researcher in the following words:

> The criticism of the EFCC...need not be waved aside, but studied...The most relevant question is: How should the EFCC be studied or investigated and analyzed? This is both a simple and at the same time a very complex question. It is simple in the sense that it is posed in such a way as to ordinarily elicit an instant, mechanically determined answer. Critically viewed, it is rather complex and its complexity is most likely attributed to the nature

of the Nigerian society, and more technically, "the nature of the subject matter"... There is analytically speaking, a spate of theoretical (and methodological) confusion with respect to what the EFCC is, and how it goes about performing its mandate... The form of chosen analysis makes available some basic concepts, which are indispensable to a thorough, scientific research... The purpose of analysis especially in trying to expose all the minute properties that are to be explained is to make for a holistic understanding...For any theoretical/conceptual formulation to be able to serve the purpose of the analysis of socially determined events, it must, as a condition, be suitable to what it hopes to explain... Intellectual discourse is relevant to the extent to which it is comprehensive... (comprehensible, scientific, methodical and utilitarian) ... This is the essence of scholarship. (Salami, 2007:108-122).

Source and method of data collection

Data were collected in an eclectic manner from a battery of public and private sources and content scrutinized and analysed to yield a robust and expected research study outcome. Generally, data were collected from official documents, newspaper reports and vast materials surfed from the internet from stakeholders, scholars and civil society groups, etc. Information was also drawn from the literature on the EFCC, EFCC official documents and findings on relevant studies.

Surfing the internet yielded a list of published works on the agency: periodicals containing articles, research reports, commentaries, newspaper write-ups, research notes and other materials considered germane to the study. These materials were reviewed, surveyed, examined and scrutinized with focus placed on lead articles and scholarly research reports.

Indeed, surfing the internet yielded the following over 100 contextually relevant documents which were consulted and analysed for their contextual germaneness: Economic and Financial Crimes Commission –

- Wikipedia, the free encyclopaedia; Bankole vs EFCC: Dilemma of Nigeria's Legal Process;
- allAfrica.com: Nigeria: EFCC, ICPC Lack Capacity to Investigate;
    - EFCC, Conjecture and the rule of law;
    - Nigeria: UK on EFCC and President Yar'Adua; EFCC: Nigeria on Cybercrime top ten list;
    - EFCC: Another Nigerian Disaster;
    - EFCC Blames Nigeria Woes on Corruptions;
    - EFCC Helps Wikileads Expose Nigerian Looters – in Nigeria;
    - naijaface: EFCC Nigeria; EFCC and Nigeria's own sphinx;
    - What is the full meaning of EFCC;
    - Gary Henry, EFCC, Nigeria Anti-Fraud International;
    - EFCC and Nigeria Failed The Test: All Their Pretences Were Shattered; Director Operations EFCC – Nigerian Financial Intelligence Unit;
    - Nigeria's EFCC Waning Anti-Corruption War;
    - EFCC and Nigeria Anti-Corruption War;
    - Between EFCC and 'Corrupt' Politicians;
    - EFCC: Between Perception and Reality;
    - US Solicits More Powers for EFCC to fight crime;
    - EFCC and Plea-Bargaining Issue in Nigeria: Matters Arising Currently;

24

- And the EFCC Goofed;
- Stealing Nigeria Blind and Failure of EFCC to stop thieves;
- Nigeria: Why EFCC Can't Try Ex-Leaders; Summary Report;
- Everywhere (EFCC, ICPC, CCB) stink;
- EFCC – Transparency Nigeria;
- Discredited EFCC: Another Nigerian Disaster; Corruption in Nigeria – The EFCC and Government;
- Re: EFCC, Corruption and the rest of us;
- The Nigerian LNG Project Corruption – The EFCC;
- Nigeria: AGF: EFCC and ICPC see no Evil, Do no Evil, Lot no Evil, Major Problem of EFCC in Nigeria;
- How Dare you criticize Nigerian EFCC?;
- The EFCC: Thy Glory O Nigeria;
- EFCC vs Corruption in Nigeria;
- Nigeria: Corruption – EFCC Blame Judiciary for slow impact;
- Ibori: The EFCC and the Future of Nigeria's Anti-Corruption Crusade;
- The Role of EFCC in Restoring Nigeria's Past Glory;
- A Letter to Mrs. Farida Waziri;
- Download EFCC; Problems of EFCC and Corruption in Nigeria;
- The UK-Nigeria Remittance Corridor;
- Anti-Corruption Policies in Nigeria;
- How would you rate EFCC at eight?; and
- What is the role of EFCC on Nigeria's Economy?

Newspapers reports, because of their currency, were also included. The materials were examined by thoroughly reading through them, isolating and analyzing their content or what they are all about.

In sum, content and context relevant materials and sources were consulted and utilized in the study. These included but were not limited to: statutes, texts, documents, journal publications, new reports, newspaper write-ups and other materials collected over a period of time. As indicated earlier, internet sources were employed to complement other sources of data and information. In addition, several legal statutes, federal laws, instruments, codes were also indispensable in the research. These sources included but also were not limited to: The 1999 Nigerian Constitution; The Corrupt Practices and Other Related Offences Act 2000; The Miscellaneous Offences Act; The Failed Bank — Recovery of Debt — Financial Malpractices in Bank Act 2004; Money Laundering (Amendment Act) 2004; and The EFCC (Establishment Act) 2004. United Nations and its related or affiliated agency documents were also invaluable to the research.

It was hoped that the use of this method in combination with other approaches provided useful but holistic and general view of the activities of the EFCC.

Method of data analysis

In the social and management sciences, library resources, library researches, qualitative, content and documentary analyses are acceptable research methods. It is what is generally referred to as *Descriptive Research*. Indeed, the procedures described above exemplify that concept and the procedures that were followed in the study. The procedures are quite similar to those of Bain

(1962), Oromaner (1968 and 1969), Shichor (1982) and Igbinovia (1984).

In this regard, Shichor opines that such an approach is important in research because it helps the researcher to know the subject matter and the general focus of a discourse. In sum, he concludes that reading through documentaries and other primary materials help the researcher to learn something about the organization or subject of his study; and from such endeavours, a researcher can glean needed or required vital data or information for use where such information or data would otherwise have been difficult to get, obtain, garner, harness or harvest. The same point was canvassed by Miracle (1981) whose study involved the aforementioned procedures and analytical processes.

Rationale, benefits and challenges

By its very nature, therefore, and for good or bad, the EFCC has been from its birth a most contentious, controversial, dreaded and news-generating organization whose activities are documented or reported in the popular media almost on a daily basis. Indeed, the agency has become a news-generating body. Its various activities are freely commented upon by journalists, academics, lawyers, the public, interest groups, civil society groups, human rights organizations, legal and judicial bodies, official news-bulletins and news conferences of senior officials of the EFCC, suspects, victims and other stakeholders and sundry individuals and entities, etc.

The benefits of these various batteries of commentaries in the public domain are that they afford us the opportunity to tap and rely upon them for our study-purpose in order to obtain a somewhat holistic view and assessment of the agency.

The interesting thing about these sources is that the various commentaries and opinions are freely espoused or given by opponents and proponents and other interested in-between persons so that the data or information that are gleaned cannot be said to be one-sided or altogether biased or unreliable as to confound the findings of the study.

One can safely conclude, perhaps, that in view of the inaccessibility of researcher to the EFCC and the secrecy attending or surrounding its works, activities and operations; and the general uncooperative posture and attitude of its officials to research enquiries and scrutiny, that the methods we have adopted in this study, despite its flaws and in the circumstance, perhaps, still offer the best way to gauge, study, and make some preliminary and tentative general statements about the functional performance of the agency. In sum, no matter the short-comings of this process, considerable reliance was placed on the various scattered accounts on the agency in this study: all things considered, it is the best option available in the prevailing circumstance.

One of the methodological approaches used in this study is akin to the approach adopted by Global Integrity, a Washington-based international organization to track governance and corruption trends globally (38 countries) in the last decade. Their findings are annually published in *The Global Integrity Report*. The Report assesses the accountability mechanisms and transparency measures in place or not in place in the various countries to prevent corruption through what it calls "Integrity Indicators". The indicators have six main categories as follows: Civil Society, Public Information and Media; Elections; Government Accountability; Administration and Civil Service; and Oversight and Regulation) (see Chapter Five: The Performance of the EFCC as seen in a Conclusive

Context of this book) as well as journalistic reporting of corruption. The Global Integrity approach is credible, scientific and accepted in the social science circles.

To recap, Global Integrity, the 2008 award winning Washington, D.C. based organization provides empirically supported documents which analyse the corruption trends around the globe using local resources, transparent source data and journalistic and media outlets rather than perception survey to monitor corruption and corruption worldwide. Its method or approach represents one of the world's comprehensive data analysis of the phenomenon of its concern through aggregated process of appraising organizations and incorporation of qualitative approaches which provide contextual information and actionable data (Duncan, 2006:131-161) using a blend of social service and journalistic writings to evaluate and report on the *de jure* as well as the *de facto* reality of the situation under study, like the performance of the EFCC.

It also produces GI Report, an annual collection of original, in-depth national assessments combining journalistic reporting with 300 "Integrity Indicators" analyzing the institutional framework underpinning countries' corruption and accountability system.

Global Integrity and the United Nations Development Programme also recommend combining a rigorous literature review with other original qualitative methods to appraise organizations (June et al, 2008). It's reporting is overwhelmingly cited by most newspapers worldwide, and is used by the World Bank, USAID, Millennium Challenge Corporation and other donor agencies to evaluate aid priorities.

To underscore the research importance of the methodological approach, it was given an award in 2008 for its earth-breaking methodological approach. In 2009, the approach was utilized to compile comprehensive data which covered these 38 countries: Algeria, Armenia, Azerbaijan, Bosnia-Herzegovina, Brazil, China, Columbia, Georgia, Ghana, India, Indonesia, Lebanon, Macedonia, Malawi, Mexico, Mongolia, Nepal, Nicaragua, Norway, Qatar, Rwanda, Serbia, Sierra Leone, Slovakia, South Korea, Syria, Trinidad, Uganda, Ukraine, United Arab Emirate, United States, Venezuela, Vietnam and Zimbabwe. The regional breakdown were as follows:

8 : Sub-Sahara Africa
4 : East and Southeast Asia
7 : Europe
5 : Latin America
6 : Middle East and Central Africa
6 : South and Central Asia
2 : North America and Caribbean

A modified version of the Global Integrity index was used in this study to partly and partially provide the intellectual foundation approach to assess and appraise the performance of the EFCC in Nigeria (See 5:11).

Indeed, there is no better way of performing the assessment or appraisal of the EFCC, an organization whose activities are classified as confidential and whose operations are shrouded in secrecy (Nigeria's rising, 2011:17), than combining this approach with a batteries of other approaches.

What is important, perhaps, is that at the end of the study, a robust research was effectuated, a robust outcome was achieved, and an equally robust understanding and credible appraisal of the performance of the EFCC was enhanced and obtained. In addition, knowledge was advanced, delivered and promoted by the research undertaking. The research study tried to overcome the flaws detected by coming as close as practically possible to the ideal standard of report findings. Indeed, it is hoped that the study contributed to knowledge in the subject–area and helped reduce the dearth of scientific literature and scholarly discourse in the area. By way of summation: we think our general inferences were reasonable in the light of our own and others' experience in Nigeria and elsewhere although we cannot assign a precise exactitude to that conviction. The point is succinctly and aptly put by Brew (2001:186):

> Research must acknowledge its disasters as well as its achievements; its rigidities as well as its creativity; its power and its powerlessness; its openness and its dogmatic blinkers.

Chapter 4

Historical background, legal status and organisational structure of the EFCC

Background to the discourse

The background story of the creation of the EFCC is an interesting and sad one. Between 1990 to 2002, Nigeria was in the limelight as a nation of crimes and criminals. The situation became so bad that the image of the country received bashing around the world: Nigeria lost respect among the comity of nations; Nigeria was blacklisted and Nigerians were tagged as criminals around the globe; some foreign investors avoided doing business with Nigeria; foreign governments and business concerns refused to invest in Nigeria and the country was brought low and in disrepute.

From year to year, the country was ranked at the top of the most corrupt countries in the universe. For example, as at June 27, 2001, Transparency International (TI), ranked Nigeria as the second most corrupt nation in the world after Bangladesh, and in 1999, the country was second only to Cameroon on the corruption index. But by June 2000, Nigeria had moved up the scale to knock Cameroon off the number one spot (Return, 2002:17). Transparency International had for two consecutive years (1996 – 1997) also rated Nigeria the most corrupt country in the world (see Tables 1 and 2).

Similarly, Nigeria was ranked the second most corrupt country in the world after Bangladesh in reports published by Transparency International on 28th August, 2002 and October 2, 2003 (Nigeria second, 2002:1-2). (See Table 1).

Furthermore, at a symposium on international fraud in Lagos in 1992, Interpol reported that bank frauds involving Nigerians represented 42% of all fraud cases worldwide. Many of the cases were said to have originated from Nigeria (Akintunde, 1994:10). Similarly, in 1991 Britain alone reported no fewer than 25,000 cases involving Nigerian tricksters (Much Ado, 1992:18). Indeed, because of the ingenuity of Nigerians in perpetrating fraud, a British newspaper reported: "the Nigerian elite is a truly criminal caste whose crookery spreads far and beyond its national borders...Nigerians are also believed to be behind a substantial social security fraud in the United Kingdom" (They Must, 1995:12). Another tabloid went on to describe Nigerians as "the evil geniuses" (Nigerians, 1993:5). In commenting on these happenings, a Nigerian said:

> With advance fee fraud mush-rooming into a major industry... people no doubt have set for us the image of fraudsters on a level perhaps unprecedented in global notoriety (Utomi, 1995:25).

The level referred to above was defined aptly by an American, General Collin Powell. Of Nigerians, he said:

> Nigeria is a nation of (120) million people, with enormous wealth. And what they could have done with the wealth over the last twenty years... they just pissed it away. They just tend not to be honest. Nigerians as a group, frankly, are marvellous scammers. I mean it is in their national culture (Powell, 1995).

Note must be made that corruption has a destabilizing effect on political and economic systems. Corruption undermines the foundations of sustainable development in all developing countries, including Nigeria. Indeed, political fallout from corruption creates a vicious circle of more corruption, instability, weak institutions, and even more corruption. This sustains the cycle of poverty endured by so many in Nigeria. Alluding to this, the Nigerian Catholic Secretariat Forum said: "Corruption is responsible in large measure for the broken promises, the dashed hopes and the shallow dreams that have characterized the existence of Nigerians in the last few decades" (On Corruption, 2002:56). Indeed, no aspect of Nigerian life is spared.

According to the Chairman of Transparency International, "Political elites and their cronies continue to take kickbacks at every opportunity. Hand in glove with corrupt business people they are trapping whole nations in poverty and hampering sustainable development." Indeed, Thomas L. Friedman seem to confirm this fact when he described Nigeria as a full-fledged kleptocracy because it is a state built around theft (Asemota, 2002:6). Regrettably, Nigeria has worn this medal of shame for more than three decades (Akaridi, 2003:39).

This is what President Olusegun Obasanjo said about the corrupt situation in Nigeria during his inaugural address to the nation on May 29, 1999. He said:

> The impact of corruption is so rampant and has earned Nigeria a very bad image at home and abroad. Besides, it has distorted and retrogressed development. Our infrastructures – NEPA, NITEL, ROADS, RAILWAYS, EDUCATION, HOUSING and other social services were allowed to decay and collapse – Government officials

became progressively indifferent to propriety of conduct and showed little commitment to promoting the general welfare of the people and the public good. Government and all its agencies became thoroughly corrupt and reckless. Members of the public had to bribe their way through in Ministries and parastatals to get attention and one government had to bribe another government agency to obtain the release of their statutory allocation of funds.

It was the sordid situation like those detailed in the foregoing narrative and graphically captured in Tables 1, 2, 3, 4, 5 below that impelled the Olusegun Obasanjo government (1999 – 2007) to establish and give birth to the EFCC to combat the menace. To sum up the situation, Ribadu said:

...When you think of "corruption", there will always be specific personalities and places that jump (come) to mind, and inevitably Nigeria is near the top of that list...

Between 1960 and 1999, Nigerian officials had stolen or wasted more than $440 billion. That is six times the Marshall plan, the total sum needed to rebuild a devastated Europe in the aftermath of the Second World War. When you look across a nation and a continent riddled with poverty and weak institutions, and you think of what this money could have done – only then can you truly understand the crime of corruption, and the almost inhuman indifference that is required by those who wield it for personal gain (Ribadu, 2009:153).

Table 1: *Transparency International's Ten Most Corrupt Nations in the World as at 28/8/2002*

1. Bangladesh (1.2)
2. Nigeria (1.6)
3. Angola (1.7
   Madagascar (1.7)
   Paraguay (1.7)
4. Indonesia (1.9)
   Kenya (1.9)
5. Azerbaijan (2.0)
6. Uganda (2.1)
7. Moldova (2.1)

Countries are given a score out of a possible perfect 10.

Source: "Nigeria Second Most Corrupt Nation". Vanguard, August 29, 2002:1-12.

Table 2: *Transparency International's Most Corrupt Three Nations in the World (1999 – 2003)*

Country	Year 1999	Year 2000	Year 2001	Year 2002	Year 2003
Nigeria	2nd	1st	2nd	2nd	2nd
Cameroon	1st	2nd			
Bangladesh			1st	1st	1st

Source: Igbinovia, P.E. (2003). "The Criminal In All of Us: Whose Ox Have We Not Taken." University of Benin 71st Inaugural Lecture Series.

37

Table 3: *Bank Fraud in Nigeria from 1989 to 1999*

Year	Amount Involved (Naira-Million)	Actual/Expected Loss	No. of Staff Terminated/Retired/ Dismissed for Fraud
1989	105.0	15.3	313
1990	804.2	55.8	417
1991	388.6	26.7	514
1992	411.8	73.1	436
1993	1,419.1	246.4	516
1994	3,399.4	950	737
1995	1,011.4	229.1	625
1996	1,600.7	375.3	552
1997	3,777.9	226.54	566
1998	3,129.3	623.50	311
1999	6,367.7	2,713.4	596

Source: "CBN, NDIC Differ Over Fraud Cases in Banks". *The Guardian,* September 2, 2002:3.

Table 4: *Forgery and Fraud Cases in Nigerian Banks: 2000 – 2001*

	2000	Amount Involved 2000	2001	Amount Involved 2001
CBN	908	₦2.53 billion ₦7.78 billion ₦1.02 million	908	Various sums of money.
NDIC	403	₦2.83 billion Loss (₦1.081 billion)	943	₦11.244 billion Loss (₦906.3 million)

Source: "CBN, NDIC Differ Over Fraud Cases in Banks".
The Guardian, September 2, 2002:3.

Table 5: *Amount of Money Allegedly Misappropriated in Federal Government Ministries in 2001*

S/No.	Ministry	Amount Misappropriated
1.	Cooperation and Integration in Africa	₦10,453,573,241.81
2.	Power and Steel	₦ 4,394,649,602.19
3.	Works and Housing	₦ 2,262,797,737.01
4.	Defence	₦ 1,785,877,023.15
5.	Education	₦ 1,265,272,388.99
6.	Police Affairs	₦ 1,209,216,327.05
7.	Information	₦ 664,124,321.46
8.	Commerce	₦ 640,053,177.72
9.	Health	₦ 465,103,959.12
10.	Industry	₦ 356,064,369.12
Total		**₦23,860,732,145.20**

Source: Atojoko, S. (2003). "Rape of a Nation". *Newswatch*, February 24:26).

History and rationale for the establishment of the EFCC

The pressing need to stem the monumental spate of or pervasive corruption and unbridled incidence of economic and financial crimes in Nigeria and the need to launder the domestic, and especially, the international image of the country which was severally battered around the world and its consequential and attendant effects on national development, growth and progress; necessitated the creation or establishment, first of the ICPC in 2000 and secondly, of the EFCC in 2002 (enacted) and 2004 (amended Act) by the President Olusegun Obasanjo administration of 1999 to 2007.

The ICPC was created to tackle the problem of corruption and related matters while the EFCC was to fight the problem of economic and financial crimes and related practices. The two bodies were created as separate and autonomous but complementary, and as we shall see later, role-conflicting, competing and rival bodies.

Note must be made here that the government's desire to establish the agencies was not fully and altogether informed or impelled by nationalistic or patriotic or altruistic flavour. In part, these agencies were created to meet the demands of the government to keep its house in order if it was to benefit from the international community and to be a respected member of the comity of nations, especially when Nigeria was ranked in successive years in the top echelon of the most corrupt and graft-infested countries in the world. This embarrassing situation vitiated national development and brought the nation to international odium and opprobrium, according to the United Nations, G-8 countries, Transparency International (TI) and other donor countries. In sum, as far as the international community was concerned, it was not going to be business as usual: Nigeria was expected or required to get its acts together by rooting out those malfeasances or at least stemming or ameliorating them if it was going to be a beneficiary of financial opportunities/donations, business investments and foreign capital support.

The establishment of the EFCC, therefore, was impelled by social, political and economic expediency and imperatives. Indeed, the coming into being of the EFCC was due mainly to the pressure from the international community on Nigeria to do something about its image and the all-pervading nefarious crime and corruption situation in the country. The country was required to do something to stem the tide or risk losing foreign investments and financial support. In commenting on these developments, the EFCC *Handbook* stated:

> Prior to the establishment of the EFCC, economic and financial crimes constituted a great challenge to the Nigerian economy and its image profile. For more than a decade, the country became a safe haven for perpetrators of Economic and Financial Crimes. Fraudulent activities, economic mismanagement, corruption, lack of accountability and transparency have been the bane of the economy. The administration of President Olusegun Obasanjo has therefore demonstrated a strong political will to fight economic and financial crimes by reposting the country to the path of sustainable development. The EFCC was established pursuant to these objectives as the financial watchdog of the business environment, with the mandate to sanitize the system (Handbook, 2004:1).

In March 2011, a similar comment was made by the former Executive Chairman of the EFCC, Farida Waziri:

> Before the anti-corruption regime of the last couple of years which has brought Nigeria to international spotlight, poverty, unemployment and poor infrastructural development remain a common decimal in both the public and private life of the nation. Her major challenge and albatross has been the issue of corruption and its debilitating appendages – bribery, graft, fraud, manipulations and nepotism. Hence, the general assumptions and position amongst economic pundits and international stakeholders is that corruption is indeed the

bane of Nigeria's development as a people and as a society. Its attendant effects have been so deep-seated that it has stunted growth in all sectors of Nigeria's socio-economic life. Against this backdrop, the investments apathy arisen from the fear of being conned by intending foreign investors and the attendant high rate of poverty and stunted economic growth has made the need for an increased capital flow to Africa a huge challenge.

Over the years, Nigeria's external image suffered setbacks as it consistently remained the world's second most corrupt nation in the world in 2000, 2001 and 2002 (TI, 2005), it moved to the sixth position, showing a positive but minimal dive towards an improvement of sort but obviously still remains among the most corrupt nations of the world. This development earned Nigeria a stigma in the international community with a considerable apathy against her economic environment as the world became reluctant to invest in Nigeria for fear of fraud. Suffice to say, the low turn of investment locally and internationally has culminated into gross unemployment and poverty engendered by economic mismanagement and endemic corruption. It is therefore imperative to state that the escalating rates of poverty in the country caused by poorly implemented economic policies, misappropriation of funds, among others, culminated in state and mass poverty, the fear of which drives people to capitalize on opportunities for self enrichment. Closely related is the societal pressure exerted on the public office holders and few affluent individuals by members of their nuclear and extended families to help them in one way or the other to survive the scourge of poverty. Hence, misappropriations of funds across the rungs of public institutions pervade the nation's public sector. Although, corruption and financial crimes are not peculiar to Nigeria, they are global phenomena bedevilling almost all the countries of the world. Corruption related crimes such as money laundering and advance fee fraud perpetrated by Nigerians affect foreign nationals and nations that relate with our country.

Consequently, Nigeria came to be viewed with suspicion as a safe haven for global criminals and a conduit pipe for the manufacture, orchestration and exportation of crimes such as money laundering and internet scam hence the abysmal low level of capital flow from foreign investment with its tolls on the Africa continent.

It was against this background that the civilian administration of President Olusegun Obasanjo instituted the anti-corruption campaign with the establishment of the Independent Corrupt Practices and Other Related Offences Commission, ICPC and later the Economic and Financial Crimes Commission (EFCC) to among other things, curb corruption and other forms of economic crimes and sanitize the Nigerian business environment with a principal object of attracting investors to the country and indeed Africa. (Waziri, 2011:1-2).

On the other hand, Salami captured the EFCC history with a political slant:

The argument here is that the EFCC is a strategic formulation of former President Obasanjo aimed not only to deal with perceived enemies, subdue and make them responsive to his political machinations and calculations, but is as well a device to enable Nigeria receive the good rating of the international community. EFCC is therefore an impressionistic outfit or a caricature policy of Nigeria's external image redemption. It is a make-believe that "things are getting better" in Nigeria (Salami, 2007:111).

While the BBC (British Broadcasting Corporation) concluded:

The EFCC was established... partially in response to pressure from the Financial Action Task Force on Money Laundering (FATF), which named Nigeria as one of 23 countries non-cooperative in the international community's efforts to fight money laundering (Nigeria Arrests, 2005).

Waziri exactly made the same point recently when she wrote that "by 2002, Nigeria found its way in the Financial Action Task Force's list of Non-Cooperative Countries and one of the conditions for being taken off that list was compliance with Recommendation 26 of the FATF's then 49 recommendations which required the creation of a Financial Intelligence Unit" (2011b:1).

Legal status and organizational structure of the EFCC

The EFCC (Establishment) Act was enacted in the year 2002 by the National Assembly. The Act was repealed in 2004 and a new Act came into force as the Financial Crimes Commission (Establishment, etc) Act 2004. It commenced operation on April 16,2003.

As we have seen, the EFCC was created to launder Nigeria's image and sanitize the Nigerian economic and social environment which was plagued and continues to be plagued by the menace of economic and financial crimes.

The enabling Act has seven parts: Part I deals with the creation of the EFCC; Part II deals with its functions; Part III focuses on appointment of staff and staff regulations; Part IV creates offences; Part V deals with the forfeiture of assets of persons arrested for offences against the Act; Part VI focuses on the financial provisions of the EFCC while Part VII deals with miscellaneous matters.

For the purposes of this book, we shall be mainly concerned with Sections 1 to 13: Part I, II, and III of the Act because of their relevance and importance to the central concern of the study: a holistic appraisal of the EFCC. The sections provide for the following:

PART I

Establishment of the Economic and Financial Crimes Commission, etc

1. **Establishment of the Economic and Financial Crimes Commission**

   (1) There is established a body to be known as the Economic and Financial Crimes Commission (in this Act referred to "The Commission") which shall be constituted in accordance with and shall have such functions as are conferred on it by this Act.

   (2) The Commission –

   (a) shall be a body corporate with perpetual succession and a common seal;

   (b) may sue and be sued in its corporate name and may, for the purposes of its functions, acquire, hold or dispose of property (whether movable or immovable);

(c) is the designated Financial Intelligence Unit (FIU) in Nigeria, which is charged with the responsibility of co-ordinating the various institutions involved in the fight against money laundering and enforcement of all laws dealing with economic and financial crimes in Nigeria.

2. Composition of the Commission

(1) The Commission shall consist of the following members–

(a) a Chairman who shall –

   (i) be the chief executive and accounting officer of the Commission;

   (ii) be a serving or retired member of any government security or law enforcement agency not below the rank of Assistant-Commissioner of Police or equivalent; and

   (iii) possess not less than 15 years cognate experience;

(b) the Governor of the Central Bank of Nigeria or his representative; and a representative each of the following Federal Ministries –

   (i) Foreign Affairs;

   (ii) Finance;

   (iii) Justice;

(d) the Chairman, National Drug Law Enforcement Agency or his representative;

(e) the Director-General of

    (i) the National Intelligence Agency or his representative;

    (ii) the Department of State Security Services or his representative;

(f) the Registrar-General, of the Corporate Affairs Commission or his representative;

(g) the Director-General, Securities and Exchange Commission or his representative

(h) the Managing Director, Nigeria Deposit Insurance Corporation or his representative;

(i) the Commissioner for Insurance or his representative;

(j) the Postmaster-General of the Nigeria Postal Service or his representative;

(k) the Chairman, Nigerian Communications Commission or his representative;

(l) the Comptroller-General, Nigeria Customs Service or his representative;

(m) the Comptroller-General, Nigeria Immigration Service or his representative;

(n) the Inspector-General of Police or his representative;

(o) four eminent Nigerians with cognate experience in any of the following, that is, finance, banking, law or accounting; and

(p) the Secretary to the Commission who shall be the head of administration.

(2) The members of the Commission, other than the Chairman and the Secretary, shall be part-time members.

(3)　The Chairman and members of the Commission other than ex officio members shall be appointed by the President and the appointment shall be subject to confirmation of the Senate.

3.　Tenure of office

(1) The Chairman and members of the Commission other than ex officio members shall hold office for a period of four years and may be re-appointed for a further term of four years and no more.

(2) A member of the Commission may at any time be removed by the President for inability to discharge the functions of his office (whether arising from infirmity of mind or body or any other cause) or for misconduct or if the President is satisfied that it is not in the interest of the Commission or the interest of the public that the member should continue in office.

(3) A member of the Commission may resign his membership by notice in writing addressed to the President and that member shall, on the date of the receipt of the notice by the President, cease to be a member.

4.　Vacancy in membership

Where a vacancy occurs in the membership of the Commission, it shall be filled by the appointment of a successor to hold office for the remainder of the term of office of his predecessor, so however that the successor shall represent the same interest as his predecessor.

5. Standing orders

The Commission may make standing orders regulating its proceedings or those of any of its committees.

PART II

Functions of the Commission

6. Functions of the Commission

The Commission shall be responsible for -

(a) the enforcement and the due administration of the provisions of this Act;

(b) the investigation of all financial crimes including advance fee fraud, money laundering, counterfeiting, illegal charge transfers, futures market fraud, fraudulent encashment of negotiable instruments, computer credit card fraud, contract scam, etc.;

(c) the co-ordination and enforcement of all economic and financial crimes laws and enforcement functions conferred on any other person or authority;

(d) the addition of measures to identify, trace, freeze, confiscate or seize proceeds derived from terrorist activities, economic and financial crime related offences or the properties the value of which corresponds to such proceeds;

(e) the adoption of measures to eradicate the commission of economic and financial crimes;

(f) the adoption of measures which include co-ordinated preventative and regulatory actions, introduction and maintenance of investigative and control techniques on the prevention of economic and financial related crimes;

(g) the facilitation of rapid exchange of scientific and technical information and the conduct of joint operations geared towards the eradication of economic and financial crimes;

(h) the examination and investigation of all reported cases of economic and financial crimes with a view to identifying individuals, corporate bodies or groups involved;

(i) the determination of the extent of financial loss and such other losses by government, private individuals or organisations;

(j) collaborating with government bodies both within and outside Nigeria carrying on functions wholly or in part analogous with those of the Commission concerning –

   (i) the identification, determination of the whereabouts and activities of persons suspected of being involved in economic and financial crimes;

   (ii) the movement of proceeds or properties derived from the commission of economic and financial and other related crimes;

51

(iii) the exchange of personnel or other experts;

(iv) the establishment and maintenance of a system for monitoring international economic and financial crimes in order to identify suspicious transactions and persons involved;

(v) maintaining data, statistics, records and reports on persons, organisations, proceeds, properties, documents or other items or assets involved in economic and financial crimes;

(vi) undertaking research and similar works with a view to determining the manifestation, extent, magnitude and effects of economic and financial crimes and advising government on appropriate intervention measures for combating same;

(k) dealing with matters connected with extradition, deportation and mutual legal or other assistance between Nigeria and any other country involving economic and financial crimes;

(l) the collection of all reports relating to suspicious financial transactions, analyse and disseminate to all relevant government agencies;

(m) taking charge of, supervising, controlling, co-ordinating all the responsibilities, functions and activities relating to the current investigation and prosecution of all offences connected with or relating to economic and financial crimes;

(n) the co-ordination of all existing, economic and financial crimes investigating units in Nigeria;

(o) maintaining a liaison with the office of the Attorney-General of the Federation, the Nigerian Custom Service, the Immigration and Prison Service Board, the Central Bank of Nigeria, the Nigerian Deposit Insurance Corporation, the National Drug Law Enforcement Agency, all government security and law enforcement agencies and such other financial supervisor institutions involved in the eradication of economic and financial crimes;

(p) carrying out and sustaining rigorous public enlightenment campaign against economic and financial crimes within and outside Nigeria; and

(q) Carrying out such other activities as are necessary or expedient for the full discharge of all or any of the functions conferred on it under this Act.

7. Special powers of the Commission

(1) The Commission has power to -

(a) cause investigations to be conducted as to whether any person, corporate body or organisation has committed an offence under this Act or other law relating to economic and financial crimes;

(b) cause investigations to be conducted into the properties of any person if it appears to the Commission that the person's lifestyle and extent of the properties are not justified by his source of income.

(2) In addition to the powers conferred on the Commission by this Act, the Commission shall be the co-ordinating agency for the enforcement of the provisions of –

(a) the Money Laundering Act, 2004; 2003 No. 7,1995 No. 13;

(b) the Advance Fee Fraud and Other Related Offences Act, 1995;

(c) the Failed Banks (Recovery of Debt and Financial Malpractices in Banks) Act, as amended;

(d) the Banks and Other Financial Institutions Act, 1991, as amended;

(e) the Miscellaneous Offences Act; and

(f) any other law or regulation relating to economic and financial crimes, including the Criminal Code and Penal Code.

PART III

Staff of the Commission

8. Appointment of Secretary and other staff of the Commission

(1) There is established for the Commission a secretariat which shall be headed by the Secretary who shall be appointed by the President.

(2) The Secretary shall be -

(a) the head of the Secretariat of the Commission;

(b) responsible for the administration of the Secretariat and the keeping of the books and records of the Commission;

       (c) appointed for a term of five years in the first instance and may be re-appointed for a further term of five years subject to satisfactory performance; and

       (d) subject to the supervision and control of the Chairman and the Commission.

(3) The Commission may, from time to time, appoint such other staff or second officers from government security or law enforcement agencies or such other private or public service as it may deem necessary to assist the Commission in the performance of its functions under this Act.

(4) The staff of the Commission appointed under subsection (3) of this section, shall be appointed upon such terms and conditions as the Commission may, after consultation with the Federal Civil Service Commission, determine.

(5) For the purpose of carrying out or enforcing the provisions of this Act, all officers of the Commission involved in the enforcement of the provisions of this Act shall have the same powers, authorities and privileges (including power to bear arms) as are given by law to members of the Nigerian Police.

9. Staff regulations

(1) The Commission may, subject to the provisions of this Act, make staff regulations relating generally to the

conditions of service of the employees of the Commission and without prejudice to the generality of the foregoing, the regulations may provide for-

(a) the appointment, promotion and disciplinary control (including dismissal) of employees of the Commission; and

(b) appeals by such employees against dismissal or other disciplinary measures, and until the regulations are made, any instrument relating to the conditions of service of officers in the Civil Service of the Federation shall be applicable, with such modifications as may be necessary, to the employees of the Commission.

(2) Staff regulations made under subsection (1) of this section shall not have effect until approved by the Commission, and when so approved the regulations may not be published in the *Gazette* but the Commission shall cause them to be brought to the notice of all affected persons in such manner as it may, from time to time, determine.

10. Pensions

(1) Service in the Commission shall be public service for the purposes of the Pensions Act and, accordingly, officers and other persons employed in the Commission shall in respect of their service in the

Commission, be entitled to pension, gratuities and other retirement benefits as are prescribed thereunder, so however that nothing in this Act shall prevent the appointment of a person to any office on terms which preclude the grant of a pension or gratuity in respect to that office.

[L.F.N. 2004 Cap. P4.]

(2) For the purposes of the application of the provisions of the Pensions Act any power exercisable under the Act by a Minister or other authority of the Government of the Federation (not being the power to make regulations under section 23 thereof) is hereby vested in and shall be exercisable by the Commission and not by any other person or authority.

11. Training programme

The Commission shall initiate, develop or improve specific training programmes for its law enforcement and other personnel charged with responsibility for the eradication of offences created by this Act and such programme shall include–

(a) methods used in the detection of offences created under this Act;

(b) techniques used by persons involved in offences created under this Act and appropriate counter-measures;

(c) detection and monitoring of the movement of proceeds and property derived from economic and financial crimes intended to be used in the commission of offences under this Act;

(d) methods used for the transfer, concealment or disguise of such proceeds, property and instruments;

(e) collection of evidence;

(f) law enforcement techniques;

(g) legal prosecution and defence; and

(h) dissemination of information on economic and financial crimes and related offences.

12. Establishment of special units, etc.

(1) For the effective conduct of the functions of the Commission, there may be established for the Commission the following units -

(a) the General and Assets Investigation Unit;

(b) the Legal and Prosecution Unit;

(c) the Research Unit;

(d) the Administration Unit; and

(e) the Training Unit.

(2) Notwithstanding the provisions of subsection (1) of this section, the Commission has power to set up any unit or committee as may be necessary to assist the Commission in the performance of its duties and functions under this Act.

13. Special duties of the units

(1) The General and Assets Investigation Unit shall be charged with the responsibility for-

(a) the prevention and detection of offences in violation of the provisions of this Act;

(b) the arrest and apprehension of economic and financial crimes perpetrators;

(c) the investigation of assets and properties of persons arrested for committing any offence under this Act;

(d) the identification and tracing of proceeds and properties involved in any offence under this Act and the forfeiture of such proceeds and properties to the Federal Government;

(e) dealing with matters connected with extradition and mutual assistance in criminal matters involving economic and financial crimes.

(2) The Legal and Prosecution Unit shall be charged with the responsibility for -

(a) prosecuting offenders under this Act;

(b) supporting the General Assets Investigating Unit by providing the unit with legal advice and assistance whenever it is required;

(c) conducting such proceedings as may be necessary towards the recovery

59

of any assets or property forfeited under this Act;

(d) performing such other legal duties as the Commission may refer to it, from time, to time.

(3) There shall be appointed for each of the Units a principal officer who shall be known by such designation as the Commission may determine.

Part IV, Sections 14 to 18 of the Act details the major offences of major concern to the EFCC as: offences relating to financial malpractices; offences in relation to terrorism; offences relating to false information; retention of proceeds of a criminal conduct; and offences in relation to economic and financial crimes.

As the name and nomenclature implies, the EFCC is essentially an anti-graft outfit concerned with economic and financial crimes. Under the laws establishing it, certain aspects of crimes that may relate to matters like terrorism, bombing and corruption also fall within its mandate.

Chapter 5

Appraisal of the performance of the EFCC as seen in multiple contexts

This chapter sets out to answer a few basic questions: What was the EFCC set out to achieve? How well has the agency achieved its objectives or what has the agency achieved since its establishment? What are those factors militating against the performance of the agency or what has been the problems and constraints which have impeded the performance of the organization? How can these factors or constraints be addressed or remedied to enhance the performance of the agency? Have the achievements of the agency outweighed its weaknesses or failures and vice versa or has it been a mixed grill? Indeed, has the EFCC been able to achieve or perform satisfactorily those functions which the Act setting it up mandated it to pursue and attain? The answers to these questions are pointers or indicators as to whether the EFCC has met the objectives why it was created. In sum, the answers to these questions constitute the basis of the appraisal of the performance of the EFCC.

A comprehensive and holistic appraisal of the performance of the EFCC was carried out based on the following multiple (eleven) level-factors: the performance of the EFCC as seen in the EFCC, Presidency, public, research and sundry contexts. In addition, the EFCC was also appraised in terms of how the enabling Act, plea-bargaining, electoral process and other factors had impacted negatively or positively on the performance of the agency.

The performance of the EFCC as seen in the EFCC context

In a "Testimony before the House Financial Services Committee" in the United States on May 19, 2009 titled: "Capital Loss and Corruption: The Example of Nigeria", Nuhu Ribadu, the pioneer Chairman of the EFCC, catalogued the following things as constituting the achievements of the agency during his 5-year tenure:

(1) "Building the EFCC into a world-class crime fighting agency with trusted partnership with US and UK agencies."

(2). Before the EFCC was formed, Nigeria had *"never secured a single criminal conviction for corruption charges"* But during his tenure, by 2007, the agency had *"secured convictions for corruption charges"*. Also, by 2007, the agency had *"secured convictions in over 275 of the near 1000 cases in the courts"*.

(3). The EFCC *"paved the way for a far-reaching banking reform in the country"* and for *"the consolidation of about a hundred mushroom banks into 25 strong banks"*.

(4). The EFCC helped to address the problem in the Niger Delta by making sure *"money meant to have gone for development"* did not go to very corrupt individuals; and *"in 2003-2004, almost 100,000 barrels of oil was stolen daily"* but by 2005-2006, the EFCC had managed to reduce this to 10,000 per day. The EFCC also secured convictions for kidnappers in the Delta, who were driving the circle of violence and bribery with the oil companies.

(5). The EFCC had helped to initiate statutes to stem corruption in Nigeria.

He concluded by saying that his "modest" success at the EFCC was supported by efforts of institutions of the United Nations, regional bodies, and many bilateral bodies like the U.S. Secret Service, the FBI, the U.S. Postal Service, and the Department of Justice, among others (Ribadu, 2009).

Buttressing these achievements, Bello-Imam indicated that although the EFCC is in its embryonic years [2002 – 2005] of existence, it has made a number of significant progress vis-a-vis its mandate. According to him, eleven of its most significant achievements are as follows:

i.   The Commission between May 2003 and June 2004 recovered money and assets derived from crime worth over $700 million. It also recovered another £3 million pound sterling from the British Government.

ii.   It arrested virtually all the notorious Advance Fee Fraud kingpins operating in Nigeria. Out of this number, about 500 suspects are in its custody and most of them are standing trial in the various courts in the country.

iii. It is presently prosecuting well over 100 cases in court and investigating over 500 cases which are in various stages.

iv.   It is presently prosecuting one of the biggest world fraud cases involving about $242 million arising from a bank fraud in Brazil.

v.   It has increased the revenue profile of the nation by about 20% due to its activities in the Federal Inland Revenue Service and the Seaports.

vi.   It has recovered revenue of over ₦20 billion from fraudsters for the government treasury.

vii. It has played a key role in the government reform programmes, e.g. restructuring of the Nigeria Customs Service.

viii. It has recovered billions of Naira for the government in respect of failed government contracts.

ix.   It has curbed oil bunkering in the Niger Delta Region. The initial daily illegal bunkering of about 300,000 – 500,000 barrels has now been substantially reduced to anything less than 50 thousand barrels.

x.   It is presently prosecuting over 20 persons involved in the vandalisation of oil pipelines. (Ribadu; 2005;9).

xi.   As a mark of its universal positive approval, the EFCC has procured grants of 20 million Euros for three years from the European Union and 3 million USA dollars from the World Bank to assist it in capacity building, purchase of telecommunication equipment and specific training in investigative techniques. The Commission has also enjoyed immense goodwill from both U.K and U.S.A.

Concluding, Bello-Imam opined that the emerging dividend from the achievement of the EFCC today is that corruption and other financial crimes are not only being audaciously put in check, the business environment and specifically the banking sector is being sanitised with a view to enhancing both accountability and transparency in both government and private business. [Bello-Imam, 2005:229-230].

Some of these achievements seem to find some support. In 2008, President George Bush of the United States said of the EFCC: "The EFCC has seized millions in the proceeds of crime, anti-money laundering efforts have been successful and Nigeria is cooperating with the international community to improve its efforts against laundering even more" (Aiming, 2008:39).

Similarly, in a paper presented by the former Chairman of the EFCC, Farida Waziri, at the United Nations Conference on Least Developed Countries in Istanbul, Turkey in 2011, she opines that the agency, during her tenure, has "vigorously pursued its mandate of investigating and disseminating information to all relevant agencies all over the world on economic and financial crimes." She claimed that the EFCC recorded successes in several areas of its mandate. She went on to list the areas as followings:

(a)   The advent of the EFCC impacted positively on the country's global acceptance by being a turning point in the country's anti-corruption resulting in attracting foreign investors and laundering the country's image.

(b)   The EFCC recorded several prosecutions and convictions on corruption, money laundering, oil pipeline vandalism and related offences.

       These prosecutions and convictions include those involving corrupt top public offenders and top government functionaries like a former Inspector General of Police, former President of the Senate, State Governors, Ministers and Parliamentarians, etc.

(c)   The EFCC recovered assets and money worth over $6 billion from corrupt officials and their cohorts. The agency is also currently dealing with over 65 high-profile cases and over 1500 other cases in Nigerian Courts. In addition; it secured over 600 convictions including the prosecution of one of the biggest fraud cases in the world involving about $242 million bank fraud in Brazil (see Tables 6 & 7).

(d)   The EFCC helped to increase the revenue profile of Nigeria due to its collaboration with the Federal Inland Revenue Service and the Seaports which led to the recovery in excess of ₦75 billion (over $500 million).

(e)   The EFCC helped to cleanse and sanitize the Nigerian banking sector through investigation and prosecution of top officials and others for money laundering and other frauds.

(g)   The EFCC helped to restore confidence in Financial Institutions and the Sock Market. This resulted in the boosting of local and international confidence in the country's financial sector and led to the country gaining more points in the Transparency International's global corruption perception index.

(h)   The EFCC helped to stem the incidence of bank failures which was rampant in the country leading to the recovery of over $5 billion bad loans.

(i)   The EFCC was in the forefront in the re-organization of critical agencies of government such as the Police, Customs and the NDLEA. The EFCC took the credit for the removal from office of the leadership of these institutions for corruption.

(j)   The EFCC facilitated the recovery and return of proceeds of Advance Fee Fraud (419) crimes and the attendant prosecutions and convictions of key operators.

(k)   The EFCC promoted partnership with Microsoft against Internet Scam and Identity theft. This helped to combat cyber crimes and led to the development of appropriate software to effectively address the problem.

(l)   The EFCC helped to promote capacity-building for law enforcement and judicial officials to better equip them to fight corruption. The EFCC also helped to foster training for designated judges handling cases within the EFCC mandate.

(m)   The EFCC promoted the sensitization of the public on the menace of corruption, sponsored public campaign and whistle-blowing programmes to ensure that Nigeria buy-in to the anti-corruption fight through the Anti-corruption Revolution Campaign (ANCOR).

(n)   The EFCC contributed to the success of the 2011 General elections nationwide which had been adjudged as one of the freest in the nation's history.

(o)   The EFCC fostered economic and political stability in Nigeria and drummed up support for the enforcement of the anti-graft laws and other regulations relating to transparency and accountability by public officers to help curb corruption in governance. This led to a measure of stability in the economic and political landscape.

(p)   The EFCC encouraged the passage of anti-terrorism laws to stem terrorism financing and money laundering which had portrayed Nigeria in bad light among the comity of nations.

Concluding the narration of her achievements, Waziri said: "It is obvious that the EFCC has remained a major anti-corruption agency in the country's fight against corruption"

(Waziri, 2011a:1-6). Indeed, some other noticeable achievements of the EFCC under the former Chairman, according to reports, are the continued battle against corruption epitomized by the arraignments of some people hitherto considered as untouchables in Nigeria: Iyabo Obasanjo-Bello , Kenny Martins, El-Rufai, Bode George, Femi Fani-kayode, Babalola Aborishade, Dimeji Bankole, etc., who have been variously charged for corruption by the agency. Even the EFCC itself opined that it has also hired four Senior Advocates of Nigeria (SANs), among other lawyers, to strengthen the Commission's legal team (Anti-Corruption, 2008:37).

Table 6: *Record of EFCC Related Investigations and Convictions from 2003 to 2011*

S/N	Class of Cases	Convictions	Under Trial	Under Investigations
1.	Politically exposed persons/high profile cases	36	75	105
2.	Advance fee fraud (419)	428	789	445
3.	Money laundering	15	163	26
4.	Cyber crime/ internet fraud	137	26	186
	Total	616	1503	762

Table 7: *Record of EFCC Recoveries from June 2008 to March 2011*

S/N	Sector	Naira Value	Dollar Value
1.	Banking	₦650 Billion	$4.3 Billion
2.	Taxation	₦3.5 Billion	$23.3 Billion
3.	Local business/firms	₦150 Billion	$10 Million
4.	Multi-national penalties	₦36 Billion	$240 Million
5.	Others: Forfeitures, advance fee fraud, etc.	₦135.5 Billion	$903.3 Million
	Total	**₦975 Billion**	**$6,500,000,000**

Source: Modified by researcher from undated and untitled paper presented by F. Farida (2011), Executive Chairman, The EFCC, at the United Nations Conference On Least Development Countries (LDC-IV), Istanbul, Turkey.

Farida Waziri's essay above is almost a complete replica of the May 16, 2011 paper she presented to the Nigeria – British Chamber of Commerce (2011b). The only departure is the presentation of Table 8 below which she claims shows that the EFCC during her tenure was not in the business of witch-hunting or thwarting or truncating the political ambition of opponents of government as was previously the norm. She indicated that this impartiality was impelled by the EFCC's decision "to stay away from the political terrain and concentrate on educating the masses which has invariable led to the rejection" at the 2011 polls of those the EFCC were alleged to be investigating and prosecuting (see Table 8).

Table 8: *Politically Exposed Persons (PEPs) Standing Trial Who Contested During the 2007 and 2011 Polls*

	PEPs Standing Trial	During 2007 Polls	During 2011 Polls
1.	PEPs standing trial and contested election.	14	15
2.	Ex-Governors standing trial, contested and won.	7	2
3.	Ex-Governors standing trial, contested and lost.	0	7
4.	Other PEPs standing trial, contested and won.	7	3
5.	Other PEPs standing trial, contested and lost.	0	12
	Total	**28**	**39**

Source: Waziri, F. (2011b). "The EFCC's Critical Role in Growing the Economy". May 16.

The performance of the EFCC under President Olusegun Obasanjo

President Olusegun Obasanjo, the initiator and creator of the EFCC ruled Nigeria from 1999 to 2007. Under his regime, the EFCC detained and prosecuted (some would say, persecuted) people outside the provisions of relevant laws. The rule of law appeared to have been bastardized and suspects were investigated and pronounced guilty without even going through court processes. People were tried selectively and the agency operated "like a loose cannon or a servile blood hound in the hand of a vengeful master out to settle scores with perceived enemies" (Aondoakaa: The AGF, 2007:42). Indeed, the regime was accused of lacking the political will to make the EFCC work; and the EFCC turned itself into a terrorist machine to hunt down political foes (Kalu, 2011:7). Alluding to this, the editorial in *The Nation* said:

> We must state that the war on corruption must continue with or without Mallam Ribadu. Ribadu's zest and energy upped the tempo of the war and focused the Nigerian on official malfeasance on a large scale. He exposed, if sometimes vaingloriously, not a few officials and that gave him an aura of a folk hero.
>
> There can be no denying the fact, though, that the EFCC under Mr. Ribadu has acquired notoriety for witch-hunting the political enemies of the *ancient regime* and trampling on the civil rights of suspects. He was the arrowhead of the most brazen and insidious assault on federalism when the agency was being used to destabilize states where the governors constituted an opposition to former President Olusegun Obasanjo.

71

Under the guise of fighting corruption, state lawmakers, usually minority elements, as against the requirement of two-thirds, were coerced to impeach their governors. The EFCC was also part of the plot to illegally block the candidature of some candidates in the last elections.

Again, while the EFCC waxed lyrical on the corrupt practices of some public holders, it was silent on the allegations made against the then President, thereby portraying the agency as a tool to clobber some persons. The implication of this is that the agency has divided reception among the Nigerian public, hardly being perceived as focused on fighting corruption.

If the President announced Mr. Ribadu's removal as EFCC chairman or retired him altogether, there would have been enough justification (Ribadu's Course, 2008: 13).

Further buttressing the point, another commentator wrote:

While Obasanjo remained in office as President, EFCC operatives proudly donned the garb of untouchables with the mandate of arresting and prosecuting all corrupt political office holders and other individuals fingered in corrupt or fraudulent acts. These they did, in the estimation of some people, with an overzealousness bordering on high-handedness and arrogance. Apart from complaints of intolerance and high-handedness, there were also accusations of selective hounding of individuals by the EFCC on political grounds but under the guise of advancing the course of the anti-corruption campaign. But the worst of these accusations bordered on what is perceived as the anti-graft agency's disregard for the rule of law in the pursuit of its mandate. Some of its critics even went as far as accusing it of often playing the accuser, the jury and the judge against those it has arrested for prosecution. (Aondoakaa, 2007: 42).

To this, Omatseye (2012:64) added:

the EFCC and ICPC... have failed in their hallowed mission. Like Charles Dickens noted, they may be light in themselves, but they give light to nothing... (The EFCC) is a charade. We all know this from inception when former President Olusegun Obasanjo turned it into a rabid Alsatian to hound and hunt his foes... The EFCC became the tool of the President; Here is where the law is manipulated either to hound enemies or to exculpate friends... the EFCC has become the tool for violating legal integrity... the EFCC and ICPC... (are) whited sepulchres (2012:64).

Indeed, in a categorical assessment, the editorial of the *Daily Sun* (2011:18) said: "During the regime of former President, Chief Olusegun Obasanjo, the agency under Ribadu was accused of partiality, witch-hunting, brazenness, and arbitrariness in its handling of the war against corruption."

With a situation like this, little wonder the pioneer Chairman of the EFCC was variously described, first, as "a loose cannon and an unguided missile which almost compromised his job under Obasanjo" (Aiming, 2008:39); and, Secondly, as a person rich "in excesses in his draconian and even partial execution of his EFCC mandate" (Ribadu's dismissal, 2009:22).

The performance of the EFCC under President Umaru Yar'adua

President Umaru Yar'Adua ruled Nigeria from 2007 to 2010. His administration was not spared from the accusation of using the EFCC as the government political machine to shield political associates and cohorts from prosecution by the EFCC and to hamper the activities of the agency in the fight against graft. Indeed, he was alleged to have fired the pioneer Chairman of the EFCC and replaced him with a stooge in order to "water corruption" (Government, 2009) and make the war against the malfeasance go "comatose" (A War Abandoned, 2008; Yar'Adua, 2008).

In the former President's first public reaction to the barrage of allegations, Yar'Adua said he "will never provide a safe haven or escape route for anyone, no matter how highly placed they may be and irrespective of whatever role they played or claim to have played in his election, if they are found to have soiled their hands by looting public funds" (Graft, 2007: 1, 15).

To compound the President's problems, the Attorney General and Justice Minister during his tenure was also accused of defending the corrupt instead of helping to fight the menace, of shirking of his responsibilities by not vigorously prosecuting public officers believed to be corrupt, of defending powerful, politically exposed persons (among them ex-governors accused of graft), of frustrating the anti-graft war, of being a cog in the wheel of the EFCC, of interfering in the agency's work and of interfering in the investigation and prosecution of corrupt people through dubious legal advice (From The Editor, 2009: 23-30). Buttressing the claims, an Editorial opinion in *Tell* said of the Attorney-General:

By his actions and utterances, the public feeling is that the man, who ought to be fighting to have those suspected of engaging in corrupt practices arraigned and tried, is the person frantically defending them. Much as Aondoakaa has tried to argue to the contrary, that perception won't go away. The people are not stupid. Neither are they blind. When they see former public officers, who they know ought to be in jail, strutting all over the land, hobnobbing at the highest levels, and even landing new multi-billion naira contracts, how can they believe there is any fight against corruption (From The Editor, 2009:8).

In spite of all these allegations, President Yar'Adua went ahead, however, to grant the Attorney General and Justice Minister the following requests that he had made:

(a)   That all agencies involved in the prosecution of criminal offences such as the EFCC and ICPC should report and initiate criminal proceedings with the consent and approval of the Attorney-General of the Federation as specified in relevant sections of the Constitution.

(b)   That the Attorney-General of the Federation exercise powers conferred on him pursuant to Section 43 of the EFCC Act 2004 to make rules or regulations with respect to the exercise of any of the duties, functions or powers of the EFCC.

The above move was interpreted by many Nigerians as an attempt of the then President and the Attorney-General to cage the EFCC which was then prosecuting some former governors for corruption. On realizing this, the Federal Government, within two days, reversed the decision saying while the Attorney-General indeed has powers of oversight over EFCC, ICPC and such bodies, he does not enjoy monopoly of power over initiating prosecution going by a subsisting Supreme Court ruling. With this, the power of the EFCC and ICPC to initiate criminal proceedings without recourse to the Office of the Attorney-General seemed, perhaps, to have been restored (How Yar'Adua, 2007:11).

In sum, taking stock of the anti-corruption policies under both the President Obasanjo and President Yar Adua's administrations, in a seminal work titled *Anti-Corruption Policies in Nigeria Under Obasanjo and Yar Adua: What To Do After 2011?*, Enweremadu (2011) concludes that the fight against corruption under these regimes were not too impressive but were marked by inefficiency, vindictiveness, unseriousness and politicization.

With specific regards to Yar Adua, the United States government "perceived his administration as one shielding the corrupt" largely because of his relationship with James Ibori, the ex-convict and ex-Governor of Delta State, "whose activities created the impression that he was above the law." On this overall impression, Olusegun Adeniyi, the former Special Adviser to the late President Umaru Yar'Adua on Communication concluded: "there is nobody to blame but the late president himself" (Adeniyi, 2011:19; 21; 38).

The performance of the EFCC under President Goodluck Jonathan

President Goodluck Jonathan became the President of Nigeria in 2010. His current tenure runs from 2011 to 2015.

Under his presidency, many commentators have alleged that he has also been shielding corrupt political office holders and public officers instead of fighting corruption. For example, in may 2011, the President of the Conference of Nigerian Political Parties (CNPP) was outraged that the Nigerian President was sitting over an Investigation Report which allegedly indicted the former Speaker of the House of Assembly (Dimeji Bankole) which the EFCC had submitted to the Nigerian President since September 2010 (Hands off, 211:13):

> Instructively, the NEXT newspaper also made the same point when it wrote:
> In one of the cases involving the (ex-speaker), and investigated by the EFCC, Mrs. Waziri, on June 7, last year (2010), told journalists her commission had submitted its report to the presidency, a claim the presidency promptly denied. All efforts to get the EFCC to make the report public or act on it failed as the commission chose to keep mum (Ndibe, 2011:55).

NEXT newspaper also reported in early June, 2011 that the EFCC dilly-dallied on the corrupt cases involving the ex-Speaker because the EFCC was prevailed upon by higher authorities to put action on hold on the arrest of the high-profile politician (Ndibe, 2011:55).

In a public statement which he issued on the whole saga, the ex-Speaker of the House of Assembly (Dimeji Bankole) urged the EFCC to desist from "trial and conviction of people suspected to have engaged in corrupt practices on the pages of newspapers", saying, "this could be translated to mean undue blackmail and intimidation" (Corruption: Civil, 2011:13). He went further to say that the way the anti-graft body had gone about the matter was "very curious and unethical" (₦10 billion, 2011:7). He concluded that the agency was "engaging in sensational prosecution and conviction on the pages of newspapers on an issue as grave as corruption" (Bankole Fault, 2011:1-2).

Reacting, the EFCC raised the alarm over an alleged plot by a high-profile suspect to launch a campaign of calumny against the agency using some members of the civil society groups. In a press release on June 1, 2011, titled "EFCC Raises Alarm over Campaign of Calumny", the agency said, among other things:

> The suspect ... has chosen to employ the services of hirelings to attack the agency and its leadership... These hirelings have been paid to stage appearances on popular television and radio stations' discussion programmes... it is also part of their plan to author newspaper advertorials and articles, all for the sole aim of rubbishing the progress being made in the anti-graft war and ultimately weaken the morale of staff of the Commission... Members of the public are therefore urged to disregard jaundiced and self-serving statements that will be coming from these elements in the days ahead (EFCC Raises. 2011:49).

When the ex-Speaker was eventually arrested by the EFCC on June 5, 2011, comments changed and became more strident from some observers. It was alleged that the EFCC was in the habit of dramatizing the arrest and trial of high-profile suspects. In commenting on the arrest of the ex-speaker, a former Governor of Ogun State said the arrest was "politically motivated" and tied to the politics of the House of Representative speakership struggle which was then about to take place (Ex-speaker's, 2011:4). The same point was made by Haruna who opined that if the former speaker "had been as good a boy of the PDP Establishment" as the Senate

President, he would have escaped the fate that had befallen him. "As it is now", he argued, "even if he is eventually acquitted by the Courts, he has suffered enough embarrassment and damage to last a life time" (Haruna, 2011:64).

Arguing along the same line, a former member of the House of Representatives also berated the EFCC for selective application of the graft law which, he said, had dragged the EFCC's reputation to the mud. He concluded:

> ...EFCC has become an attack dog for the government of the day against real or perceived dissenting voice to that of the ruling government. This show of shame was prevalent under President Olusegun Obasanjo and must not be resurrected under President Goodluck Jonathan, otherwise, no one will take any anti-graft effort of this administration seriously ...

> It is obvious that with the height of incompetency and selective applications of the anti-graft laws, President Goodluck Ebele Jonathan should ask Waziri to resign or be sacked or the National Assembly should consider repealing the enabling law since it has only been to further the misuse of power, contrary to the purpose of its establishment (Charges, 2011:4).

The ex-Speaker's father even raised the ante:

> Please tell the world that some people in government, particularly the Federal Government want to kill my son the way they killed M.K.O Abiola... My son must not die in detention the way Abiola and others died... The unorthodox way and manner in which my son was arrested ... despite his earlier agreement with the Chairman of the Commission and instalmentally charging him to Court is a pointer that the government

does not mean well for him... my son is currently in the hands of his enemies (Bankole's, 2011:3).

Considering all the diverse positions on the matter, the editorial opinion in *The Nation* cautioned that what is of paramount importance now is that:

Bankole (ex-speaker) should be given fair hearing otherwise, it will give impetus to the insinuation making the rounds that the man is being hunted for reasons other than the alleged crimes said to have been committed. This would further dent the image of the commission already perceived in certain quarters as the attack dog of the government in power, usually deployed against powerful/notable opposition. The Bankole case presents the Commission with an opportunity to correct this perception...The public is watching how the matter will end (The Bankole, 2011:13).

Following the unceremonious removal from office of Mrs. Farida Waziri as the EFCC Chairman on November 23, 2011 by the Nigerian President, Mobolaji Sanusi (2011:22) opined that "like his predecessor in office, President Jonathan is not serious about combating graft in the country because the process that made him Vice-President and later President is embedded in corruption." To this, the editorial opinion of *The Nation* concurred:

The Jonathan Presidency...has shown more naivety than sincerity in tackling what has been described as the greatest challenge to Nigeria's development and indeed, her existence. Since inauguration, the current administration has not shown any sign it wants to rein in the monster of corruption by any token... It has become apparent that President Jonathan is either not keen about tackling corruption in Nigeria or has no will to do so. Perhaps both [Exit Waziri, 2011:19].

Still on the Jonathan Presidency, a writer said:

Are you a businessman or woman with substantial dealings with the Federal Government, or a politician fiercely opposed to the sitting government at the centre and eyeing a top position in Abuja? If you are, then take heed of this warning, it is in your own interest; don't do or say anything that would make the Economic and Financial Crimes Commission (EFCC) come after you, because that would spell danger for you as the Commission appears poised once again to go after the supposed enemies of their paymaster, the Presidency... over the years, especially under Obasanjo, the agency was used effectively to fight opponents of that Presidency (Odusile, 2012:22).

"The dramatic and ignominious treatment meted out to the past two Chairmen of the Commission, Mr. Nuhu Ribadu and Mrs. Farida Waziri by two successive presidents underlies the authoritarian grip of the executive arm on the agency, which is not desirable to sustain the anti-corruption campaign" (The Criteria, 2012:14). However, following the exit of Mrs. Farida, Mr. Ibrahim Lamorde, a former Director of Operations and Acting Chairman of the agency, was appointed by President Goodluck Jonathan as the Commission's Chairman. He was confirmed as Executive Chairman of the EFCC by the Nigerian Senate on February 15, 2012 (Senate Clears: 2012:7). A few weeks later, the Police Service Commission at its 26th plenary session elevated him to the position of Deputy Commissioner of Police (DCP) from his previous position as

Assistant Commissioner of Police (ACP). Commenting on this, *The Guardian* editorial stated: "Apart from merit, part of the justification for his elevation is that there were some Assistant Commissioners of Police working under him and 'for cohesion', he was elevated. This exercise has naturally engendered mixed reactions..." The editorial then cautioned that there is the need to eliminate "emergency promotion which, as in the current episode, tends to raise questions than answers" (The Criteria, 2012:14).

Speaking in Washington, D.C. on some of these developments, the Assistant Secretary for African Affairs, Johnnie Carson, said:

> For four years, the United States scaled back our technical assistance programs to Nigeria's Economic and Financial Crimes Commission (EFCC) because we did not believe the previous leadership was committed to reform. In November, President Jonathan appointed a new Chairman to run the EFCC – the country's main anti-corruption agency. The appointment of Ibrahim Lamorde to lead the EFCC gives us confidence that the high-level corruption that has hobbled the delivery of government services will be seriously addressed. (America's Support, 2012:10).

Finally, with the ill-advised, self-serving, political impelled, paternalistic, parochial, insensitive and rather thoughtless granting of presidential pardon by Goodluck Jonathan to a patented and certified international criminal and fugitive offender, ethnic cohort and kinsman of the Nigerian President, Diepreye Alamieyeseigha, on March 12, 2013, a death blow was wittingly and unwittingly finally, completely and totally delivered on the EFCC, ICPC, CCB, other law enforcement agencies and Government efforts to ever seriously stem and tackle the corruption menace that has been the scourge, opprobrium and odium of the Nigerian state for decades. As a writer succinctly puts it:

> [The pardon] is lethal to Nigeria's sulking fight against the menace of corruption... Indeed, the Alamieyeseigha pardon-gate has once again brought to the fore the insincerity of the Jonathan administration to fighting the scourge of corruption and fraud in this country... It amounted to dragging the image of the country to the pre-EFCC days of money laundering, advanced fee fraud and impunity. The sooner President Jonathan decides to eat the humble pie, the better for the country [Maikano, 2013:22].

In commenting further on how Jonathan's pardon for men of corrupt past undermines the Economic and Financial Crimes Commission (EFCC) and encourages official sleaze, the editorial of *The Nation* said:

> For President Goodluck Jonathan it was another law in the country's annals when on Tuesday March 12, 2013 he approved presidential pardon for some Very Important Personality ex-convicts. Prominent among these was Chief Diepreye Alamieyeseigha, the former Governor of Bayelsa State...
>
> We wonder what Jonathan is teaching by such a precedent... The pardon is a big blow to a country that is under the firm grips of corruption. It is unfortunate that the Jonathan administration is fighting corruption in reverse...

In a country wanton with corruption, the show of mercy is tainted and subverted. The quality of mercy has been strained. A friend and former subordinate turns the lofty principle of the prerogative of mercy to save a friend and former boss. It is not only cronyism but also nepotism. Corruption cannot be more vile.

The Economic and Financial Crimes Commission (EFCC) seems unnecessary and its effort to corral the corrupt among us futile with this slew of pardons.

It will take some time for Nigerians to recover from the rude shock of the uncommon generosity. But if Chief Alamieyeseigha and Bulama could be pardoned, we see no reason why there should be anyone behind bars in this country for fraud and corruption. So, in the interest of fairness, the gates of our prisons should be flung open for such prisoners so they can "go and steal no more." That is the least we can learn from a government that says it is not corrupt but most of its actions point in the direction that its hands are too soiled to fight corruption [Presidential, 2013:15].

To this, Oshunkeye (2013:71) concurred:

We must all tell our President the bitter truth. We must let him know that by his action, he has driven the last nail into the coffin of Nigeria's anti-graft campaign. And if that's okay by him, he should finish the good job by further compensating Alams with a cabinet position in his government and disband the two anti-graft agencies – Economic and Financial Crimes Commission, EFCC, and the Independent Corrupt Practices and Other Related Offences Commission, ICPC. He should also award a national honour to Alamieyeseigha to boot.

One thing is certain: with the unpardonable presidential pardon, Jonathan may have, perhaps, effectively terminated the anti-corruption war in Nigeria.

The performance of the EFCC as seen in the public context

From the perception of the EFCC, the agency has performed well in carrying out its mandate. But to the vast majority of Nigerians and other stakeholders, the agency appears not to have done well: it has had a dismal performance. For example, under the Umaru Yar' Adua presidency, the agency was said to have gone into "deep slumber" and "lost steam" (Jonathan's Big, 2010).

Despite efforts made in the past to fight the corruption menace, the issue of corruption has continued to rise with Nigeria still being listed among the most corrupt nations of the world by Transparency International and other agencies (Eya, 2011:64) (see Table 9).

Table 9: *Countries surveyed in the 2010 Global Integrity Report*

Under the Goodluck Jonathan regime, despite the repeated promises he had made to fight corruption, the situation has not changed. The EFCC performance has been generally believed to be sluggish and lethargic. Numerous cases, especially those concerning ex-governors and politicians have dragged on to the extent that some of the former governors standing trial, but who are on bail, may eventually remain lastingly free from judgment. Added to this is the fact that many of the ex-governors contested and won in the 2011 April general elections, ironically, despite the former EFCC Chairman's public declaration of the plan to bar politicians indicted by the agency from contesting the elections (EFCC Please, 2011:21). On these issues, a commentator said:

> But despite the promise, quite a number of critics have expressed dissatisfaction with the performance of the Economic and Financial Crimes Commission (EFCC) under Farida Waziri. Foreign commentators have described the Waziri period in the EFCC as a long lull in the fight against corruption because apart from few cases which exhibit conspicuous political interest, the anti-graft body has done little to persuade Nigerians that it is committed to achieving its mandate (Eya, 2011:64).

Furthermore, despite the existence of the EFCC for close to 10 years, as we have seen, Nigeria still remains a by-word for corruption. Indeed, "internationally, the name or country Nigeria is synonymous with corruption of the most baneful kind" (From The Editor, 2010:7). Unhappy with the country's situation, the United States in its human rights report for 2009 described the EFCC's anti-corruption efforts as "largely ineffectual". Clarifying its position on the issue, the US report stated that: "the EFCC's inability to bring a number of corruption investigations to closure, the 2008 replacement's of its chairman; and the 2008 transfer of many its senior personnel raised questions about the government's commitment to fighting corruption" (Jonathan's Big, 2010:22). Similarly, some other commentators have also accused the EFCC of not putting in place efficient and effective measures to fight graft (Jonathan, 2011:13); and that the failure of the agency to perform optimally has been due to the way the agency's operational platform is skewed: it is designed to tackle corruption from bottom to top instead of vice versa (Kalu, 2011:75). Other stakeholders had expressed dissatisfaction with the performance under the former Chairman of the EFCC. Indeed, a Nigerian legal luminary claimed that the EFCC under Waziri's leadership has not made any significant progress in the anti-graft war and that the situation has gone from bad to worse (*Tell*, 2009:26-27).

The same point was basically made by the CDRH which accused the EFCC of not fighting corruption and of not having nothing to show for its efforts. Indeed, it claimed that the EFCC had not achieved anything of significance since inception (Corruption: Civil, 2011:3).

For sometime now, the EFCC has also come under intense criticisms and barrage of attacks for being politically biased and partisan. Indeed, it is alleged that its operations and activities are generally politically motivated. For example, recently, the pioneer Chairman of the EFCC, Nuhu Ribadu, lamented that the successes he claimed to have brought to the agency had been undone by his successor in office, saying, "all of it has now changed, like many other reform efforts in the country". He went on to add that "the entire team responsible for these successes, which was trained by a variety of agencies in the US, has been moved out of the EFCC." He then went further ahead to carpet the government for playing politics and paying lip service with the fight against corruption. He wrote:

> But the policy today in Nigeria is to use all the right rhetoric – speaking of the need for the rule of law and the fight against corruption – to cover up their campaign to completely undo the reform efforts of the previous government and so thoroughly confuse corruption as anti-corruption that no one can sort out which is any longer. This is why today, many of the law enforcement agencies that used to work hand in hand with the EFCC are no longer willing to partner with the EFCC or the Nigerian Justice Department (Ribadu, 2009).

Not done yet, Ribadu went on to castigate the government for covering up government officials, Ministers, governors, party stalwarts and other powerful individuals involved in various economic and financial crimes in the country. To buttress his claims, he referred to some cases:

(a) the former Nigerian Head of State who "took for himself between $5 -$6 billion and invested most of it in the western world",

(b) The Nigerians involved in the Halliburton/KBR and Siemens scandals who "continue to enjoy the fruits of their labours";

(c) a former Governor in Delta State who was still "one of the most powerful figures in both the ruling party and the country".

Indeed, he concluded that because of politics, "alleged culprits are going about their daily lives and even running the government by default. And yet they are still engaged from outside as equal partners in governance and development" (Ribadu, 2009).

The appointment of Mrs. F. Waziri as Chairman of the EFCC on June 6, 2008 was also mired in politics. Some stakeholders believe the removal of the pioneer Chairman and his replacement, which did not go down well with many Nigerians, was also politically motivated. For example, the editor of *Tell* magazine, noted:

> The appointment of Waziri brings into sharp relief the much speculated agenda of President Umaru Yar'Adua, to turn the anti-corruption agency into a toothless bulldog... With this appointment and the exit of Lamorde from the EFCC, the message Yar'Adua has seemingly sent to Nigerians is that the Commission has been handed over to the undertaker who will conduct the final rites of passage for the much vilified EFCC (from The Editor, 2008:8).

Contrary to the EFCC's claim that "it is not and will not be a party to the power calculus of political gladiators" and politicians, it is obvious that there have been abundant evidence that the agency, particularly from 2004 to 2008, was a willing tool of the government in power. The EFCC was used at various times to effect the impeachment and removal of then serving Council Chairmen and Governors; and to hound and hunt political opponents and perceived enemies of the government in power (No governor, 2006:15). As depicted most aptly in Cartoon No. A titled "Who will dare the President", the EFCC was like the Sword of Damacles hanging over the neck of government opponents which the President wielded or dangled at will at his enemies and political opponents (Dare, 2011:15) (see cartoon No. A).

90

Cartoon No. A: Who Will Dare The President?

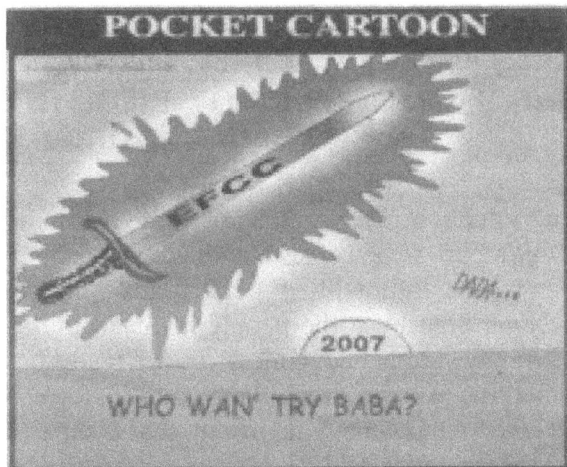

Source: Pocket Cartoon (2006). *Vanguard*, October 10:15.

Overall, the poor performance of the agency has been affected by the following factors: Its use to fight political battles or hunt political opponents of those in power; the sweeping of many corrupt cases under the carpet; the use of the agency to shield corrupt persons from prosecution; the agency's abuse of plea-bargaining; interference and uncooperative attitude of the Presidency and the Office of the Attorney-General; lack of political will by government to fight corruption; frequent leadership changes and general leadership temperament and ineptitude have all combined to slow down the work of the agency and battered its image (Jonathan's Big, 2010: 7-22).

In a sober reflection on the Nigerian situation on June 14, 2011 in far away Geneva, Switzerland, the propounder, founder and initiator of the EFCC-ICPC, Chief Olusegun Obasanjo, in a paper titled: "Meeting Sustainable Societies and Justice" which he presented at the 100th Session of the

International Labour Organisation (ILO) Conference, lamented the state of the war against corruption in Nigeria. Perhaps, the best summary to end this discussion, is ironically offered by him in this damning verdict that the Nigerian government, albeit, the EFCC, are NOT FIGHTING CORRUPTION:

> If you are going to fight corruption, it is not a one night or one day war. You have to be consistent and persistent with it. I haven't seen that will of persistency and consistency in Nigeria because the people involved in corruption are strongly entrenched. Unless you are ready to confront them at the point of even giving your life for it, then you will give in and when you give in, that is the end of it. (Government not, 2011:2).

A final note on the matter is provided by a Nigerian columnist:

> ... Obasanjo was right when he said his successor lacked the 'will' to fight corruption. What he didn't add was that even he that had the 'will' soon polluted the good works of the Economic and Financial Crimes Commission, EFCC, ... and turned it into a Gestapo Organization hounding real and perceived enemies of government. Were it not for his interference, the agency would have grown... The EFCC... can yet achieve its full mandate if the powers-that- be would let it be. Will they? (Osagie, 2011:55).

Reflecting on all these, *Tell* concluded that the EFCC has had a "lacklustre performance" and was a "publicly detested" agency [No Tears, 2011: 7, 32-33]. And *The News* magazine concurred saying the EFCC has been "an anti-corruption watchdog without fangs". It argued that "a lot of public funds go into financing the agency with nothing to show for it". It described the EFCC's attempt at tackling corruption "laughable" [The Fall, 2011:18-19].

The performance of the EFCC as seen from variegated contexts

There have been many factors which have affected the performance of the EFCC since its creation and which have made the agency unable to realize its mandate. An important constraint has been the frequent changes in the agency's leadership and direction with attendant turbulence, upheaval and uncertainty in the organization. For example, the EFCC was established approximately close to ten years ago. From 2002 to 2012, the agency has experienced three leadership changes.

The pioneer head, Nuhu Ribadu ran the EFCC from 2002 to 2008; Ibrahim Lamorde was in change in an acting capacity from January 2008 to June 2008; while another former Chairman, Farida Waziri held the position from June 6, 2008 till November 23, 2011 with Lamorde again appointed as Acting Chairman. Processes were in place in January 2012 to make him the substantive Chairman of the EFCC. Indeed, on February 15, 2012, the Nigerian Senate confirmed him as Chairman. Lamorde is the only person to have twice served as Director of Operations and Acting Chairman: an appalling average of three years tenure for three occupants. These developments have affected stability and continuity in the agency.

Apart from this, the frequent changes in leadership have also led to ill feelings, allegations and counter-allegations levelled against each successive head and their cohorts. The situation had also degenerated into unwarranted negative publicity both for the agency and the staff. For instance, when the former Chairman [Mrs. F. Waziri] took over the reins of leadership from her predecessor, she claimed that the predecessor had not properly handed over to her the instruments of office. To compound the matter, the predecessors [Ribadu and Lamorde] were alleged to have taken away some vital and sensitive files on pending investigations. On this controversy, *Tell* editorial said: "the current controversy on missing case files looks like part of a bigger agenda to castrate the agency" (A war, 2008:8).

In a related development, the leadership of the EFCC has been mired in one controversy or the other, even to the extent that the pioneer Chairman was ignominiously removed from office and the other (his brief successor) held suspect for a period. Under these successive leaderships, therefore, the EFCC had been involved in one upheaval or the other, often resulting in almost a total change of personnel, replacement and deployment of key and experienced hands, thereby leaving the operations of the agency disrupted, supine and sometimes comatose. A comment on this development is instructive:

> The other name of the Economic and Financial Crimes Commission, EFCC, seems to be controversy. It cannot be otherwise. For an agency is seen through the prism of the leadership... Her middle name (Farida Waziri) might as well be controversy. Like her predecessor, Nuhu Ribadu, whose actions were almost trailed by controversy (A war, 2008:8, 94).

The former Chairman of the EFCC, Mrs. Farida Waziri, was unceremoniously removed from office by the President on 23rd November, 2011 without stating reasons for the sack.

However, the forces that worked against the former EFCC boss were identified as the United States and British governments, the Nigerian Presidency, National Assembly, Gombe State Government, the Judiciary, the Office of the Attorney-General and Minister of Justice, aggrieved staff of the EFCC, Civil Society and Human Rights groups, victims, the general public, etc. (Nwosu, 2011: 14-15). Other sundry allegations on why she was relieved of her job included the fact that she was said to be in constant squabbles with her staff and senior subordinates, allegations of unethical conduct and procedural blunders in her prosecution of the anti-corruption war levelled against her, face-off with the Attorney General and Minister of Justice, loss of credibility of EFCC under her leadership and her actions and utterances in public (Why Farida Waziri, 2011:6). It was even insinuated in some quarters that she was also corrupt (see Cartoon B). The various comments that attended her sack in this regard are quite instructive:

> A Lagos lawyer and human rights activist offered this opinion:
> As far as I am concerned, Waziri's removal is good riddance to bad rubbish. I have never agreed with her inhuman *modus operandi* nor being her fan in her not too cleverly veiled shoddy relationship and hobnobbing with many of the nation's tainted political elite. Hers was selective justice, a dispensation that lacked human face but wore the hideous monstrous visage of persecution rather than prosecution... She relished in the grandeur of power and its effluents... the EFCC under Mrs. Farida Waziri was an oppressive and repressive machine of dubious pedigree (Jonathan Sacks 2011:5).

Arguing along the same line, the editorial opinion of *The Nation* said:

The sack of Mrs. Farida Waziri, Chairman of the Economic and Financial Crimes Commission is a mere splash in the puddle... the graft war may have been further recessed into the darker corners of the administration where not much light shines. Surely, nobody would score Mrs. Waziri excellent in her three and half-year tenure for showing much character or diligence in the fight against Nigeria's biggest ogre-corruption (Exit Waziri, 2011:19).

To this, the *Vanguard* editorial concurred:

[Mrs. Waziri's] appointment on 18 May, 2008 was steeped in a maze... Speculations were rife that she was part of a team that some politicians installed to ensure the anti-corruption campaign assumed standards that would favour some suspects... At most times, it was easier to forget EFCC existed... EFCC, from the beginning has been another of several government agencies that serve the interests of those in power. It does little else (Farida-Nothing, 2011:18).

Cartoon B: Corruption and EFCC Chairman's Tenure Elongation

Source: *Vanguard*, December 4, 2011:7.

Perhaps, the most damning and damaging comment on the whole development was recently tendered by the former U.S. Secretary of State, Mrs. Hillary Clinton who applauded the removal of the Chairman of the EFCC, and by the current U.S. Ambassador to Nigeria, Terence McCulley, who also applauded the change of leadership at the agency, saying in early December 2011:

> I applaud President Goodluck Jonathan's recent move to change the leadership of the EFCC, and his willingness to seek a strong candidate to lead the independent commission to prevent corruption and other related offenses. The US stands ready to help build these institutions to address corruption effectively and make impunity a thing of the past (US Applauds, 2011:7).

Perhaps, the best summary of the circumstances surrounding the matter has been offered by Obi (2011:56). He said:

Now if we put together the circumstances surrounding the fall of Farida as well as that of Ribadu, we will come to appreciate the fact that Nigeria is ruled by a Brotherhood. By this I mean that there is a clique of secret and powerful operators who determine, at all times, what the fate of Nigeria must be. They are faceless and nameless, yet their presence looms large in the Nigerian firmament...

If Nigeria were to be a property, you can say that they are the owners of the property. When anybody happens upon the political scene, what they do is to watch you from the rear. They size you up and gauge your response mechanism. When they want anything, they will quietly approach you and tell you what must be done. More often than not, you may ignore them because you have a naïve understanding or appreciation of who owns Nigeria. Even when you realise that they are powerful, you may continue to rebuff them because you believe that you are answerable to the big boss that appointed you. Because you are a neophyte in the undercurrents of Nigerian affairs, you wouldn't know that even the president defers to them. The reality is that you have ignored them at your peril. But that is understandable. Reality is always a late dawn...

Even when all the facts are available to you, it is possible that you may call their bluff. You would convince yourself that you have to do that if Nigeria must be rescued from the vice grip of those who want to pull it down. But you will never succeed. Nobody has ever succeeded in wrestling successfully with the Brotherhood that rules Nigeria. It is a secret operation and its modus operandi is only understood by those who know the direction that Nigeria must face at any point in time. Farida has lost her battle with this Brotherhood...

Now that Farida has lost the battle, the Brotherhood is brow-beating the commission and whatever that is left of it. They are waiting for the next boss of the EFCC. They just hope that he or she will be wise enough to read the handwriting on the wall. But that is usually a tough task. Such handwritings are never written in everybody's language. They are usually coded. Your survival begins with your ability to encode and decode. That, in itself, is enough cause for worry. All the same, we wait for the next man (or woman) who will become the unfortunate target of the Brotherhood. (Obi, 2011:56).

Another constraint on the performance of the EFCC has been its inability to cooperate and collaborate with like or similar agencies in the country. More profound, perhaps, has been the role-conflict between the EFCC, ICPC and Code of Conduct Commission (CCC). For example, sometimes ago, the EFCC transferred some case files to the ICPC on some former state governors it was investigating. The transfer of file was at the instance of the Presidency which directed the EFCC to concentrate its attention on fighting money laundering and terrorism. The Presidency did this to strengthen the operations of the EFCC and ICPC following complaints against the EFCC that it had been acting wrongly outside its mandate to the detriment of suspected offenders (EFCC Now, 2007:1,15). A human rights lawyer and activist offered this comment on the development:

I can tell you categorically that the EFCC on many occasions exceeds its legal mandates continually... We have now seen the EFCC that does everything, including debt recovery. It is too dangerous (The AG, 2009:26).

Related to this is the fact that the EFCC takes on too much tasks outside its mandate, is short-staffed, overstretched, spread-thin over the country and is saddled with too much workload, most of it self-imposed and self-impelled.

Furthermore, the EFCC has not been able to partner enough with the other related agencies in the fight against graft and corruption. Rather, there is ample evidence of unhealthy rivalry, undue duplication of functions, competition, in-fighting and turf-fighting among the agencies. For example, the government acceded to the request of the Attorney General and Minister of Justice in 2007 to ensure better coordination among the agencies and avoid untidy multiple criminal prosecutions as were then being undertaken by the EFCC, ICPC and the Code of Conduct Tribunal in respect of the same alleged offences (Graft, 2007:15). The situation still remains the same in 2012.

Similarly, the government, the police and other security agencies often also work at cross-purposes with the EFCC. For example, the government and the police were accused of shielding the ex-Speaker of the House of Representatives from EFCC arrest in June 2011 for alleged graft. Recently, *The Nation* noted:

> It was learnt that all attempts by the EFCC operatives to gain access to him were resisted by a detachment of policemen, including, some members of the Police Mobile Force.

> But the EFCC operatives laid siege to the Asokoro residence overnight with Bankole holed up inside.

> It was gathered that were it not for restraint, the EFCC operatives and policemen attached to Bankole were (about to be) engaging in a shoot-out following insistence by the operatives to gain entrance... the intervention of

(the Inspector General of Police) was said to have strengthened security around the (ex) Speaker with the EFCC displeased about the development (Alleged N10b, 2011:2).

Furthermore, a simmering quarrel broke out between the EFCC and the ICPC in 2008 following an initiative by the then Chairman of the EFCC to co-opt Ministries, Departments and Agencies (MDAs) of government into the agency's anti-corruption campaign. The EFCC Chairman's office had issued a memo to all government establishments requesting for the reactivation of the Anti-corruption Transparency Committee (ACTC) in the agencies.

However, the ICPC quickly kicked against this initiative, noting in an advertisement published in many Nigerian newspapers, that ICPC had already "established 300 Anti-Corruption and Transparency Monitoring Units (ACTUs) in all ministries, departments and agencies". The ICPC directed MDAs to disregard the EFCC directive and adhere only to its own instructions concerning Anti-Corruption and Transparency Monitoring Units. The stand of the ICPC was that such a directive amounted to duplication of efforts (A War, 2008:35-36).

One other challenge that is confronting the EFCC is the issue of funding. Funding the agency has been poor. Because of the alleged role of the erstwhile Attorney General of Nigeria for not supporting the anti-graft war in the country, particularly during the presidency of Umaru Yar'Adua, the financial support the EFCC was getting from abroad dried up and was largely terminated. Officially, the Federal Government has not given more funding to the agency (Government Action, 2009:25). Indeed, from 2008 to 2010, the EFCC battled challenges posed by inadequate resources (foreign donors left following alleged lack-lustre performance), indiscipline, internal corruption, interference from the Attorney General's Office, abuse of court processes by suspects' lawyers and frustration by politicians who tried to influence trials (Jonathan's Big, 2010:20). To compound the problem of the EFCC, the agency has also been experiencing logistic problems particularly in the number of operation vehicles and in the payment of staff salaries (Jonathan's Big, 2010:21).

The EFCC has often also indicated that the country's judiciary system had impaired and continues to impair its work and slowed down its operations making the agency to be unable to be pro-active. In an interview in 2008, the EFCC revealed that one of the greatest challenges facing it was the "slow judicial system" (Anti-corruption, 2008:37).

On the flip side of the coin, the EFCC is constantly accused of disobeying court orders in respect of criminal cases involving suspects and their spouses. For example, in a case involving the prosecution of some ex-bank directors, the agency shunned the court order issued by a judge ordering it to immediately release an ex-bank director from detention pending the final determination of a fundamental rights suit filed before the court. Similarly, a court order made by another judge for the production of a suspect and his wife was turned down by the EFCC. The agency had also, during the tenure of Nuhu Ribadu, as Chairman, displayed this same brazen violation of the rule of law. Little wonder, *Daily Sun* tagged the events as "persecution" not prosecution (Persecution, 2011:20).

Furthermore, a critic after noting that "along the line of its horrible beginning, the EFCC remained a worsening disaster", and saying "it is safe to say that there is a near consensus on the fact that EFCC is a failure", went on to accuse the organization of dominating its top hierarchy and strategic positions with persons from the Nigerian Muslim North. As at June 7, 2011, he noted, the top staff position of the EFCC was as follows:

Table 10: *Ethno-Religious Domination of Top and Strategic Positions in the EFCC as at November 22, 2011*

	Position	Name of Officer	Police Rank	Ethnicity/ Religion/Zone
1.	Chairman	Farida Waziri	AIG (Retired)	Muslim, North
2.	Director of Operations	Ibrahim Lamorde	Commissioner of Police (CP)	Muslim, North
3.	Head of Operations (Abuja Office)	Ahmad Abdurrahmah	D.C.P.	Muslim, North
4.	Head of Operations (Lagos Office)	Rabiu Muazu	D.C.P.	Muslim, North
5.	Head of Intelligence and Special Operations Section (ISOS)	Abdul Suleiman	C.S.P.	Muslim, North
6.	Deputy (ISOS)	Bashir Abdulahi	S.P.	Muslim, North
7.	Third in Command	Ibrahim	D.S.P.	Muslim, North
8.	Head of EFCC Servicom	Ibrahim Adoke	?	Muslim, North

Source: Modification of Ugwounye (2011). "EFCC: Another Nigerian Disaster". June 7.

Making a final and concluding comments on the lopsidedness of Muslim North total dominance of the top hierarchy but important positions in the EFCC, the commentator said:

> It is important to look at the two government officials who exercise oversight functions over the EFCC from the executive arm of government. They are as follows: (a) Inspector General of Police (Hafiz) Ringim — (Muslim, North). (b) The Attorney General (Mohammed B. Adoke — (Muslim, North)... The point, however, is that in a country like Nigeria, where the Speaker of the lower Chamber of the legislature and the President of the Senate, the Chief Justice of the Country, the Ministers, etc are determined by the so-called federal character and religion-based balancing, how come that an important agency like EFCC should be staffed at the top nearly exclusively with officers from one ethnic group and members of one religion? Such a situation would naturally make people from the other ethnic groups and religion suspicious and fearful. We also understand that the way we approach crimes and punishment, and due process, could largely be influenced by our religious beliefs. In an environment where there are no sound institutional safeguards for equality before the law, people will inevitably rely to greater extent, unconsciously perhaps, on their religious values and belief system... These subtle and intricate factors of bias could be reduced if you diversify the staffing of a key institution like EFCC. Remember that the test is not really whether the officers are actually biased on religious or ethnic grounds, but rather whether there is a reasonable suspicion of bias on those grounds... Yet, the government allows EFCC top officials to be solely of one ethnicity and one religion (Ugwounye, 2011:2-5).

Note must be made, however, that on March 10, 2012, the Executive Chairman of the EFCC, who was himself confirmed by Senate into that position on February 15, 2012, named six key appointees into the agency. The appointees are Director of Operation (Chief Superintendent of Police), Mr. Olaolu Adegbite; Head of Internal Affairs Department (Assistant Commission of Police), Mr. Mohammed Wakili; Director, Planning, Policy and Statistics, Dr. David Tukura; Commandant of the EFCC Academy, Mr. Ayo Olowonihi; Acting Deputy Director, Media and Public Affairs, Mr. Osita Nwajah; and Mr. Bala Sanga (Legal Unit). (Lamorde, 2012:4; EFCC Makes, 2012:13).

Instructively, these new appointments by Ibrahim Lamorde do not still substantially alter the Muslim-North dominance of the top echelon of the EFCC.

Furthermore, on April 16, 2012, it was reported that the Federal Government of Nigeria might scrap the EFCC and 37 other agencies any moment from then based on the recommendation of the Steve Oronsaye's Presidential Committee on the Rationalization and Restructuring of Federal Government Parastatals, Commissions and Agencies. In the report, the Committee indicated that from the Nigeria Police Force (NPF) alone, four agencies, the Federal Road Safety Commission (FRSC), the EFCC, the Independent Corrupt Practices and Other Related Offences Commission (ICPC), the Nigeria Security and Civil Defence Corps (NSCD), have been created, thereby duplicating functions (EFCC, ICPC, 2012:15).

Consequently, these agencies would die should the government embrace the recommendations of the Committee. Citing the case of the EFCC and ICPC, which the Committee noted are performing the traditional functions of the police, the Chairman of the Committee observed:

that even though the two Commissions were established separately to address corruption, which the police appeared to have failed to do, successive administrations have ironically continued to appoint the Chairman of the EFCC from the Police Force while the methodology adopted by the ICPC in conducting investigations as well as the training of its personnel in investigation procedure are carried out by the Police... the point that must be reiterated is the fact that an institution is inefficient and ineffective should not be a basis for the creation of new ones... Indeed, it is a fundamental breach of acceptable practice of good public sector governance to create a new agency or institution as a response to the seeming failure or poor performance of an existing agency in order to suit political or individual interests. Such a practice has proved eventually to precipitate systemic conflicts, crises and even collapse at a substantial but avoidably high financial cost to government (Panel, 2012:1, 6, 61).

Note must be made, however, that there are indications that the United States may not support any attempt to scrap the EFCC. Reacting to the Oronsaye's recommendation in this regard, a spokeswoman in the American Embassy in Nigeria, Ms. Deborah Maclean reportedly said on April 18, 2012: "As we understand it, the Nigerian Federal Government may decide to consolidate anti-corruption agencies, rather than eliminate the important functions that they can perform" (America's Support, 2012:10).

Finally, the relationship between the EFCC and the Nigerian public is far from being cordial. This is traceable to the agency's abuse of human rights, violation of the rule of law, the arrogance of its leaders and operatives and the fear they strike into the hearts of the citizenry. Indeed, the EFCC admits that one of the greatest challenges it is facing is public cynicism about the possibility of the agency winning the war

106

on corruption (Anti-corruption, 2008:37). (Compare this position with item No. 8, Table 12 of the EFCC Performance Appraisal Index) (see The Performance of the EFCC as seen in a Conclusive Context below).

The enabling ACT and EFCC performance

There can be no gainsaying the fact that part of the problems the EFCC has had in realizing its mandate, ironic as it may seem, is the constraining and debilitating elements in the enabling Act bringing the agency into being. The main elements would be highlighted here but references would be made to other problematic Sections of the Act throughout the body of this work.

The 2004 Act has 47 Sections which is aimed at addressing the menace of economic and financial crimes in the country.

One of the first noticeable flaws in the Act is its undue treatment of offences under its mandate purely and squarely from the limited perspective of law and legality: It assumes that economic and financial crime offences can only and solely be tackled by law and law enforcement; and that the problems can be legislated and enforced away. The Act does not dwell on the social parameters, correlates or determinants of the phenomenon. To attempt to tackle the problem (financial and economic crimes) away from the standpoint of law enforcement is wishful thinking and unproductive. The EFCC would never be able to successfully fight graft and corruption until and unless the social and environmental factors that predispose people to the malfeasance are given due attention. As noted by a scholar:

> The solution to economic and financial crimes cannot be found in the existence of law alone, but in the greater effort of social transformation and rebirth (Salami, 2007: 117).

107

On another level, various Sections of the Act 2004 establishing the EFCC would need to be amended if the EFCC is to be strengthened to enable it achieve its objectives. For example, Section 2(i) (a) and 2 (i)(a)(ii) states that the Commission shall be headed by a Chairman who shall be the Chief Executive and Accounting Officer and who "shall be a serving or retired member of any government security or law enforcement agency not below the rank of Assistant Commission of Police or equivalent". Similarly, according to the Act, even though the Chairman of the EFCC is a serving Police officer, once she/he was appointed as Chairman of the EFCC, she/he ceases to take orders from the Inspector-General of Police. She/he is responsible to the President of Nigeria who appointed him/her and can only remove the Chairman in accordance with the provisions of the Act.

These provisions are not only problematic but also ridiculous and ludicrous in the extreme. For one, as recent Nigeria EFCC-Police history had shown, the appointment of a serving police officer to be the pioneer head of the EFCC created a lot of problems for the agency.

Given the enormous and "almighty" powers ceded to the EFCC Chairman under Section 4, a junior Police Officer so appointed can undermine the discipline and authority of Senior Officers in the parent security or law enforcement agency. This scenario, conflict and anomalous situation played itself out between 2006 and 2007 when the pioneer Chairman of the EFCC (Nuhu Ribadu) (then an Assistant Commissioner of Police) effected the humiliating and embarrassing arrest of his Police boss, the Inspector General of Police (Tafa Balogun).

In a timorous manner and adding salt to injury, the Chairman even announced to the whole world that he was not only more powerful than the Inspector General of Police but that he was superior to him.

The Office and position of Inspector General of Police is a creation of the Constitution unlike the EFCC which is a creation of an Act. As noted elsewhere, the police is the number one security agency in Nigeria. The EFCC, under the laws setting it up when compared and juxtaposed with the Constitutional provisions which gave birth to the Police, makes the EFCC an inferior organization to the Police. Special note must be made particularly to Chapter 1, Part 1, Section 1(i) of the 1999 Constitution which states:

> This constitution is supreme and its provisions shall have binding force on all authority and persons throughout the Federal Republic of Nigeria.

The Constitution is superior to the EFCC Act. The Police, being a creation of the Constitution, is superior to the EFCC. By extension, therefore, the Inspector General of Police is superior to the Chairman of the EFCC and his authority is supreme over that of the EFCC chairman and binding on him and not vice versa, the provisions of the EFCC Act not withstanding.

The EFCC's arrest of the Inspector-General of Police did not go down well with the other security agencies in the country, particularly the police. The eventual fall from power and the ignominious exit as Chairman of the EFCC of Nuhu Ribadu, is traceable in part, to the manner and audacity of arrest of the Police Chief who was his boss. The incident further explains why till this day, there is ill feelings, mutual suspicion, hostility and uncooperation between the Police and the EFCC. Indeed, were it not for the overt complicity, collusion and tacit support of government for the EFCC, the arrest would have been impossible or at least, it would have been resisted leading to a possible show-down or bloodbath.

On a related matter, the person who occupies the position of Chairman of the EFCC needs not necessarily be a serving or retired officer "not below the rank of Assistant Commissioner of Police or equivalent". This provision completely restricts the quality of personnel or individuals that could serve in that capacity or that could have been available to the EFCC to render qualitative and expert service. Talent is not the exclusive preserve of law enforcement and security agencies or a monopoly of its rank and file. Indeed, it can be said that there is, perhaps, more talents outside these agencies than inside them.

The work of the Chairman of the EFCC, as spelt out in the enabling Act, involves basically the coordination of the work of the agency, gathering/analyzing intelligence and synthesizing and utilizing them to achieve agency goals and objectives. These are tasks which can be done by many trained professionals and experts who do not necessarily have to be serving or retired security or law enforcement personnel. Indeed, EFCC work is more research and intellectual (intelligence) based than on physical, raw power and enforcement prowess. In sum, the whole work of the EFCC centres on the coordinating ability, intellectual and intelligence know-how and on the intellectual enterprise of the Chairman. An elucidation is in order.

A close study and scrutiny of the heads or directors of the American FBI, CIA, DCI and NSA over the years would reveal that many of those appointed into these positions have

110

professional academic backgrounds. The occupants of these positions represented and continues to be represented by the best minds that are available to the country and not because they had any law enforcement or security backgrounds.

One does not necessarily need to be serving or to have served or retired from the police or other security agencies to be an expert or professional in security or law enforcement matters. Henry Kissinger (1968-1975), Zbigniew Brzezinski (1977-1981), Condoleezza Rice (2001 to 2005), among others, are or were University Professors with academic backgrounds who at various times served as National Security Advisers (NSA) to the various Presidents of the United States. Structurally and operationally, the Director of the FBI, CIA, and DCI are all under the Office of the NSA; just as the Chairman of the ICPC, EFCC; the Director-General of the SSS, DIA, NIA; and the Inspector General of Police, etc, are structurally and operationally under the Nigerian NSA. Appointment of the Chairman of the EFCC should, therefore, be *open* to all talented, brilliant, competent and qualified Nigerians who could do the agency proud, make it good and move it forward.

In commenting on this abnormal and anomalous situation in August 2011, a commentator said:

> In fact, the law expressly excluded (those) other qualifications from consideration by specifically reserving that position for retired or serving members of the forces. The law refused, albeit curiously, to allow lawyers, judges, professors, politicians or doctors to occupy that position simply because they are lawyers or judges or professors or politicians or doctors. The law wants it only for retired or serving members of the security forces [Ugwuonye, 2011].

111

Furthermore, some comments on Sections 3(2) and 4 are in order. The Sections state as follows:

3(2) "A member of the Commission may at any time be removed by the President for inability to discharge the functions of his office (whether arising from infirmity of mind or body or any other cause) or for the Commission or the interest of the public that the member should continue in office"

4. "Where a vacancy occurs in the membership of the Commission, it shall be filled by the appointment of a successor to hold office for the remainder of the term of office of his predecessor, so however that the successor shall represent the same interest as his predecessor"

The above-quoted Sections appear to give unlimited power to the President who can hire and fire the EFCC Chairman and replace members of the Commission when vacancy exists at any time. The Sections also confer on him the powers to certify any Commission member as unable to discharge his duties or to accuse such a member with "misconduct" based on his (the President) wimps and caprices to the detriment of the nation. When the above Sections are combined with the powers of the Commission in Section 6, it becomes clear, why over the years (2004 to 2011), Nigerian Presidents have been accused of misusing the EFCC to pursue their political agenda and haunt political enemies; and why successive Chairmen of the EFCC (who appear to have unlimited powers, next only to that of the Nigerian President), abuse those powers arrogantly. These Sections defeat the noble intentions of the law and the EFCC Act. The country, Nigeria, would be better served, therefore, if the EFCC is not made to appear much more powerful and superior to the other parallel security agencies in the country in order for the EFCC to be able to get the cooperation, collaboration and support of these agencies in its fight against graft and corruption.

Similarly, to remove the bottleneck that has hampered the smooth-running and performance of the EFCC, Section 12 (1) would also need to be amended to remove the danger, conflict and dilemma of subsuming Finance under Administration.

Likewise, Section 8 (4 and 5) states, respectively: that the staff of the Commission "shall be appointed upon such terms and conditions as the Commission may, after consultation with the Federal Civil Service Commission"; and "all officers of the Commission… shall have the same powers, authorities and privileges… as are given by law to members of the Nigerian Police" make the EFCC share the same conditions of services with what obtains in the general public service and/or the Police. The EFCC, by the antecedents and rationale for its creation, should not be treated as the Police or the Civil Service. It is a special and unique organization performing unique and special functions and should be treated as such without making them appear superior to other agencies. To enable the EFCC perform optimally, therefore, the work and service conditions of its staff must be sufficiently attractive and different from what obtains in the Police and the Public Service, in order to attract quality and competent personnel into the agency; and discourage EFCC personnel from graft, corruption and other corrupting influences.

Furthermore, the enabling Act [sections 2(2), 3(2,3) and 8(1)] not only places the EFCC under the President, it also makes the agency to be subject to and dependant on Government and the political order in its operations with attendant negative consequences. This trend must be discouraged. In commenting on this anomalous situation, a commentator wrote:

> (The) EFCC is not an independent agency of government, that could discharge its duties and responsibilities without fear or favour, this is because it is the President that appoints the Chairman of EFCC, and since, the President has the power of hire and fire, the top-shot in EFCC cannot but be loyal to the President to remain in office, in a similar development, it is also the President that approves the funding for the agency, if they want to be too assertive or discharge the functions independent of the President, the President can cut them to size by starving them of funds. It is a well known fact today that, before the EFCC undertakes any task or even commences any investigation; it must sought the official imprimatur of the President; also when investigations are concluded, reports are submitted to the President for perusal; the implication of this is that, EFCC cannot do anything outside of what the President wants it to do and this has been the bane of the fight against corruption in Nigeria. There is so much deceit, lies and manipulations in the corruption debate. That is why those who claim to be spearheading the anti-graft campaign are blacker than those they say, are black (Ayobolu, 2006).

The law or Act establishing the EFCC must be amended to guarantee its independence and give it bite to be able to function optimally.

Finally, the provisions of Section 27(4) and 28 are instructive for the negative effects they portend for the fundamental human rights of Nigerians and the presumption of innocence until an accused is pronounced guilty in a court of law:

> Section 27(4) states:… "whenever the assets and properties of any person arrested under this Act are attached, the Commission shall apply to the Court for an interim forfeiture order under the provisions of this Act".

> Section 28 states in part: "When a person is arrested for an offence under this Act, the Commission shall immediately trace and attach all the assets and properties of the person acquired as a result… and shall thereafter cause to be obtained an interim attachment from the Court".

The import of this patently unjustified, unwarranted and flagrant violation of suspect's rights is far reaching and disconcerting. They inflict legal tyranny on the citizen: An arrested person's assets and properties are "attached" or seized or forfeited before ("thereafter") the Courts are approached to legalize the illegality (the "interim" forfeiture or "attachment") and not the other way round. In whatever way the provisions are looked at, the suspect or "person arrested" is in a no win situation: he is deemed to be "partially" guilty until the Courts decide otherwise. The net effect is that the suspect or "person arrested" is criminalized and adjudged an offender before he appears before the bar of justice. These provisions run counter to the Nigerian Constitution and should be amended to so reflect in order to humanize the EFCC, garner citizen cooperation for the agency, enhance EFCC performance, enable the agency realize its mandate, restore Public trust and confidence and allow the rule of law to rule and reign.

Plea bargaining and EFCC performance

One of the factors that seem to be impeding the performance and the public acceptance of the EFCC is the organization's introduction and use of the novel and alien concept of plea bargain which the agency has been deploying to arbitrate, adjudicate or settle economic and financial crimes matters.

This point was forcefully articulated by the former Chairperson of the EFCC, Farida Waziri, when she said: "you cannot be using part of the public funds you stole to set yourself free and go home to enjoy the loot. Plea bargain is used in some developed countries of the world like United States and United Kingdom but that does not make it proper choice. I never like(d) it" (Onyema, undated). On August 15, 2011, however, she seemed to contradict herself when she again said: "Plea bargain is not the best but I believe that half bread is better than none. It's better to recover some of those stolen wealth than to just allow it to go like that" (I know, 2011:6).

Plea bargain is the practice involving negotiation between prosecutor and defendant and/or attorney or lawyer, which often results in the defendant's entering of a guilty plea in exchange for the State's reduction of charges, or in the prosecutor's promise to recommend a more lenient sentence than the offender would ordinarily receive.

The EFCC has been employing plea bargaining to the extent that the Nigeria public seems to be losing confidence in the ability of the agency to fight crime without fear or favour. The perception of many Nigerians is that the process is grossly abused to the detriment of efforts to stem graft. Under the process, the rich and powerful go relatively scot-free with their loot while the poor and powerless get stiff prison terms: the rich get richer and the poor get prison.

116

Under the plea bargaining concept, the former governor of Bayelsa State (D.S.P. Alamieyeseigha), the former Inspector General of Police, (Tafa Balogun), the Managing Director and Chief Executive of Oceanic Bank, (Mrs. Cecilia Ibru) forfeited some of their hefty looted funds and got to the bargain light sentences to the chagrin of the Nigerian public. This sordid situation and the abuse of plea bargain were derisively and sarcastically depicted in a cartoon piece in *The Guardian* of June 6, 2011:14 titled "THE GAME PLAN" (see Cartoon C):

First Character: I WONDER WHY THE ANTI-CORRUPTION AGENCY IS HELL-BENT ON CAPTURING THE EX-SPEAKER.

Second Character: WELL, IT'S PART OF THE OPERATION TOTALITY.

First Character: HOW?

Second Character: IT'S GOING TO BE A DO-OR-DIE MATTER OR FIGHT-TO-FINISH.

First Character: SO, WHAT HAPPENS AFTER ALL THE FIGHT?

Second Character: EM, MAYBE PLEA BARGAIN.

Cartoon No. C: The Plea Bargain

Source: "The Game Plan" (2011:14). *The Guardian*. June 6.

The same derisive and sarcastic depiction was further shown in another cartoon piece (see Cartoon D) in *The Nation* of October 10, 2011 at page 20, thus:

News Release:	EFCC ARRESTS AKALA, DANIEL, DOMA

- THE ALLEGATION: DIVERSION AND MISAPPROPRIATION OF FUNDS;
- DANIEL – ₦58 BILLION
- AKALA – ₦25 BILLION
- DOMA – ₦18 BILLION

Character A: NOW, THE AMOUNT OF FUNDS INVOLVED IN THIS ALLEGATION WAS MENTIONED TO NIGERIANS... EXACTLY HOW MUCH IS INVOLVED IN TINUBU'S CASE?

Character B: O'L BOY, THAT ONE IS POLITICALLY MOTIVATED! WHAT YOU SHOULD WORRY ABOUT IS THE FATE OF THESE 3 EX-GOVS IF FOUND GUILTY!

Character A: I ALREADY KNOW THEIR FATE IF FOUND GUILTY!... THEY WILL NEGOTIATE *PLEA BARGAINS* AND GO HOME TO ENJOY LIFE COOLLEHH!

Character B: ?!?

Cartoon No. D: Again, The Plea Bargain

Source: Editorial/Opinion (2011). *The Nation*, October 10:20.

The same sarcasm is also shown in Cartoons E, F and G below:

Cartoon E: Yet Again, The Plea Bargain

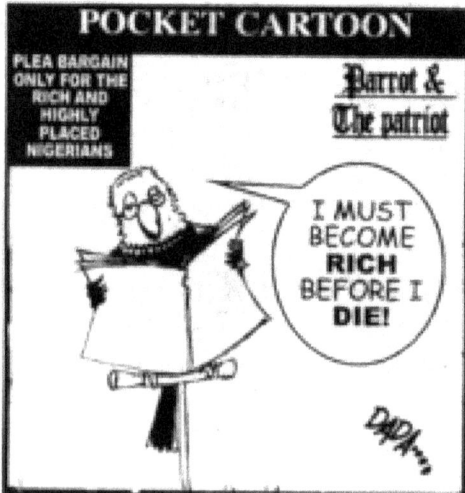

Source: *Vanguard*, April 4, 2012:5.

Cartoon F: Nigeria's Application of Plea Bargain Decries

Source: Vanguard, April 4, 2012: 18.

Cartoon G: The Notorious Armed Robber and Plea Bargain

Source: *The Nation* (2012:9). May 12.

It is instructive to note that in a public opinion survey/ poll conducted by the *Vanguard* on the use of Plea bargain by the EFCC, almost all the persons interviewed were opposed to and did not support the idea. Here is a sample of some of the opinion expressed by the respondents:

(a) "the use of plea bargain shows that the EFCC arrogates to itself some judicial powers which it does not have. It will not help the image of the EFCC. Nigerians know what is going on".

(b) "Plea Bargaining is aiding and abetting corruption. It is like we are saying 'all animals are equal but some are more equal than the others'... What is good for the goose is also good for the gander. The law does not say there should be a plea bargaining; if we continue this way, then we are not enforcing the rule of law".

(c) (Plea Bargaining) "tantamount to corruption itself".

(d) (Plea Bargaining) "is a case of preferential treatment and injustice".

(e) "EFCC is on the verge of ruining itself... the judicial process must be allowed to take its course and appropriate punishment meted out to (offenders)" (What, 2007: 16).

The official position of the EFCC with regard to the agency's curious adoption of plea bargaining has been expressed by the EFCC's former Head of Media and Publicity. Writing in the *Sunday Sun* of October 23, 2011 at page 15, he illogically said:

Even the contentious issue of plea-bargaining is not an EFCC construct. It is an issue of global jurisprudence and the local criminal justice system is only adopting it as a practical way of mitigating the effects of corruption on the polity (Babafemi, 2011:15).

Contrary to the position of the EFCC, plea bargaining is an American invention or contraption which was imported into Nigeria largely by the EFCC. It is alien to Nigerian law and does not exist in our laws, contrary to rumours. To this extent, the EFCC justification that the concept is used all over the world is ridiculous, sterile, and untenable. It is of no moment and is no argument at all.

The plea bargaining contraption is perceived by the larger Nigerian public as an attempt to shield corrupt but powerful individuals from conviction. Indeed, the former Minister of Justice and Attorney General of Nigeria and Former World Court Judge, Bola Ajibola, noted that the judicial tool called plea bargain, being used by the EFCC, amounted to corruption. He advised that the EFCC should not allow convicted politicians to enter into plea bargain. He contended that political office holders, no matter how highly placed, should serve their prison terms. He went further to opine that the use of plea bargain would be counter-productive in the war against graft and corruption as it would encourage other people to steal public money. He concluded:

> If you have stolen, let it be taken by due process, in accordance with the rule of law. Let those who are found guilty serve their terms. What is the essence of someone arrested, tried, convicted, sentenced and at the end of it you release him on plea bargaining?... (Plea Bargaining) is akin to a situation whereby you are caught by a policeman and he says if you give me money I will release you. It is part and parcel of corruption. It is still part of

extortion. The way I look at it is that I frown at the whole idea (EFCC Disagrees, 2007: 1, 15).

Plea bargaining is alien to Nigerian law and the Nigerian landscape; it is a concept and contraption forced on the nation by the EFCC. It must be jettisoned as it has negative effect on the country's jurisprudence, on the Nigerian psyche and on the public perception of the EFCC. The concept commercializes the criminal justice system; it does more harm than good to the system; is prone to abuse and misuse and is a promoter and facilitator of graft which the public condemns and abhors.

Perhaps, the best statement on the matter is offered by Onyema, who wrote:

[There are] the illogicalities embedded in the plea bargain doctrine, at least, as it affects Nigeria... [B]ased on the shameless disposition of the Nigerian public office holders... we are not developed enough to accept it in our criminal justice administration... Plea bargain will not only encourage corruption but will also constitute a financial conduit pipe for selfish and unscrupulous leaders to siphon public funds... The Nigerian public should also arise... in condemning plea bargain because of the observed idiosyncrasies of the beneficiaries of the said plea deal and those standing trial... Plea bargain can never be the best approach in treating the public office holders who loot treasuries entrusted on them... Judging from the temerity with which public fund is being looted these days and the expenditure and life style of the culprits, something more serious need to be done to deter others who intend to emulate plea bargain "beneficiaries"... For this national shame to be curbed, these known criminals,... must, apart from forfeiting their loots, spend reasonable period of time in the jail houses... Mere persuasions and/or giving them soft landing will only encourage more havoc to the society. Besides, if they are not strictly sent to jail, our youths ... based on precedent, will erroneously be following their footsteps (Onyema, undated).

A final nail on the coffin of the plea bargain concept was, perhaps, driven home on the 15th of November, 2011 by the Chief Justice of Nigeria (Justice Dahiru Musdapher) when he lambasted the use of the contraption by the EFCC in Nigeria, saying, it makes a mess of the war against corruption. He also opined that the concept was not only alien to Nigerian law, substantive and procedural, but was also a novel imposition of dubious origin which was aimed at shielding high profile crooks who stole public money by offering them soft landing. He concluded:

[Plea Bargain] was invented to provide soft landing to high profile criminals who loot the treasury entrusted to them. It is an obstacle to our fight against corruption; it should never again be mentioned in our jurisprudence (CJN Faults, 2011:64).

To this, the editorial of the *Sunday Sun* of March 11, 2012 at page 6 added:

...our view is that the practice is not in the best interest of Nigeria and the war against public corruption... (It) can only nourish public corruption that has become the bane of national development in Nigeria.

As we have said in previous editorials, *we do not support plea bargains and all other practices and laws that allow persons accused of corruption to escape justice by simply either giving up a portion of stolen sums, or at the pleasure of the Attorney General of the Federation and the president.*

Corruption is a serious problem that seriously undermines the development of Nigeria. Plea bargains can only fuel corruption. The nations should neither embrace nor encourage its practice ... We believe the interest of the country will be better served when persons accused of corruption are seen to be brought to justice, to serve as a deterrent to others. Potential treasury looters will not be deterred when persons that are guilty of corruption are only made to cough out a fraction of their loot, and thereafter left to thumb their noses at the nation and its failed criminal justice systems as they flaunt the rest of their stolen loot.

Nigeria does not need to sheepishly copy other parts of the world that practise plea-bargaining. Many of them have never experienced the level of public corruption that has pushed our country to its knees.

Nigerian authorities need to get the nation's moral compass right if we are to win the war against corruption.

Plea-bargaining is immoral. It has little redeeming value. (The Plea Bargain, 2012:6).

Similarly, on April 2, 2012, the Senate President David Mark also said that plea bargain is a tool to help the rich escape justice. He argued that it is doubtful whether plea bargain has served the cause of justice. He concluded that public perception is that plea bargain has been used not to meet the ends of justice but to protect big men, who have committed crimes far more heinous than those awaiting trials in Nigerian prisons. (Plea Bargain, 2012:9).

Arguing along the same line, the Academic Staff Union of Nigerian Universities (ASUU) commented in November, 2012 the union was opposed to giving support to criminals by asking them to part with some of the loot, adding that it does not portray the nation as serious. The union through its President opined:

> You catch somebody and tell him to bring a part of what he has stolen. It is not going to stop others but will encourage other criminals to steal. Honestly, plea bargaining is just another way used by the political class to protect its own. The stealing is mostly done by the political class. If somebody steals ₦100 million and you ask him to part with ₦60 million... what stops him from stealing ₦200 billion next time? We at ASUU do not support giving protection to criminals (ASUU Kicks, 2012:8).

On this, the Editorial of *The Nation* of September 2, 2012 at page 19, concurred:

> The government's position on this serious matter raises some issues of great concern about its anti-corruption war. The essence of the very idea of plea bargaining is corruption. The former Governor of Edo State, Lucky Igbinedion, used plea bargaining to return what was suspected to be only a fraction of his loot from the government treasury. What this tells us is that looting of government treasury is a very profitable venture in Nigeria.

> Plea bargaining is an investment that yields great profit at the end of the day. It must be a new invention of making cool money and it is antithetical to good governance, to say the least. This is probably the reason why the immediate past Chief Justice of the Federation, Aloysius Katsina-Alu condemned, in no ambiguous terms, the highly corrupt system of plea bargaining for thieving politicians and the likes in our society.

The resort to plea bargaining by indicted marketers and the Federal Government's body language of seeming approval is a clear indication that it has institutionalised corruption by using corruption to fight corruption. The result is corruption unlimited. If we are to fight corruption with all sincerity, we should at all times and in all cases fight corrupt practices with criminal prosecution in order to serve as deterrent to others, and not let offenders go away with plea bargaining.

For government to want to cover up the dirty deals of indicted marketers just because it feels their exposure to criminal activities through trials and consequent punishment would have international consequences on their dirty business is to attract to itself public outcry and condemnation. It (has) become clear to all that the fire of corruption in Nigeria has always been fuelled by the government that is supposed to quench it whenever and wherever it surfaces. (No Plea, 2012:19).

The point was further driven home by another commentator:

To a layman on the street, plea bargaining in the Nigerian context is a system in which room is provided to unfettered looting of public treasury at all levels of governance. This is done in such a way that billions of public money is stolen, and some paltry millions are returned to the coffers of the government, while a large chunk of the looted public funds at the end of the day is left for the looter and his/her unborn generations to savour.

There is no doubt, stealing of public funds will be on the increase with the acceptance of 'plea bargaining' in our judiciary system. The excuse given by the former EFCC chairman, that she saw nothing wrong in application of plea bargaining by our law courts, on the ground that it is widely accepted in advanced countries like the US and Britain will make absolute nonsense of the fight against corruption in our country. (Why Encourage, 2012:15).

Reviewing the whole situation concerning the plea bargaining contraption, Omotunde (2012:21) concluded:

From ongoing revelations on the fuel subsidy scam to capital market and pensions rip-offs, it has become evident that the fight against corruption has been mere sweet talks meant to distract. With the deluge of public fraud encamping the land, many Nigerians are not trusting the government to deal with the unrighteous circumstances as desired for the interest of the nation. People's confidence on the earnestness and sincerity of the once-feared anti-corruption agencies to deal with the nation's financial unpleasantness keeps diminishing by the day. As it were, EFCC appears to be on the path of being re-tagged Economic and Financial Crimes Compromise with the new boss Ibrahim Lamorde himself confessing that the supposed anti-fraud agency is filled with financially polluted and counterfeit minds. (Omotunde, 2012).

Repudiating their earlier stand or position on the matter, in an apparent volte-face or double-talk, the EFCC former spokesman, Mr. Femi Babafemi, said on November 18, 2011:

We have never hidden the fact that we are not uncomfortable with plea bargain... we had adopted it because of the frustration of cases going on for years without a headway... with the position of the CJN that corruption cases should no longer take more than 6 months, if strictly adhered to, then, plea bargain becomes totally unattractive for whatever reason (Our Stand, 2011).

The electoral process and EFCC role performance

The Economic and Financial Crime Commission (EFCC) was created by Act of 2004. Section 6 of Part II of the Act specifies the basic functions of the Commission. Section 6 (b and c) underscores the main functions of the Commission as follows:
The Commission shall be responsible for:

...(b) The investigation of all financial crimes including advanced fee fraud, money laundering, counterfeiting, illegal charge transfers, future market fraud, fraudulent encashment of negotiable instruments, computer credit card fraud, contract scam, etc.

(c) The coordination and enforcement of all economic and financial crime laws and enforcement functions conferred on any person or authority.

In recent years, however, the agency in the opinion of many Nigerians, appears to be operating outside its jurisdictional and investigative lenses. Indeed, the agency has on numerous occasions been accused of getting itself enmeshed in partisan politics on behalf of the ruling government in power. The allegation is that the agency had in the 2003 and 2007 elections operated outside the extant laws establishing it. Indeed, the EFCC, it is said, has no direct or specific electoral roles to play except the one it has imposed on itself as a willing tool of government. An elucidation is in order here.

In the 2003 and 2007 (not 2011) elections in Nigeria, many political actors in the opposition parties were allegedly harassed, hunted, arrested and intimidated by law enforcement and security agents, particularly, the EFCC on trump-up, politically-motivated corruption charges designed to stop, discourage, dissuade and prevent them from contesting for political slots against candidates from the ruling party. Expectedly, the ruling party candidates had a field day "winning" the elections.

The same scenario appeared to have played itself out as the country approached the 2011 general elections. For sometime, the EFCC gave a hint, although the agency later denied it, that it had a "list" of corrupt candidates who were not fit and proper to run for the various elections.

On February 24, 2011, the former Chairman of the EFCC, Mrs. F. Waziri, was reported to have said that candidates facing corrupt charges should excuse themselves from the 2011 elections, threatening that the "list" of such candidates would be made available to INEC. She went on to add that political parties candidates in their own interest with corruption cases would regret in the end if they were fielded by their parties for elections. Hear her:

> ...it will be unfortunate for any party or constituency to put forward any candidate standing trial for corruption charges and, in a short while, such a person is convicted and taken to prison. That party or constituency has lost that chance or slot (Alli, 2011:2).

This development would have had many consequences for the polity and the entire electoral process. It could have thrown the country into anarchy and confusion; it could have delayed, truncated or reduced the credibility of the poll proper;

it could have led to endless and serial litigations by aggrieved political actors and parties; it could have led to other unforeseen events that could have threatened the peace and tranquillity of the country and jeopardized its democratic drive.

Fortunately, the EFCC did not carry out its threat. Rather, it acquitted itself creditably well in the 2011 elections; and, together with the other security agencies in the country, helped to deliver a free, fair and credible elections in 2011; and in the process, helped to move the country's nascent democracy forward while enhancing the polity's democratic credence and credentials.

The role the EFCC should be playing in subsequent elections is a simple and clear one: it should be seen by all political actors and stakeholders as fair, non-partisan and strictly professional outfit. It should restrict itself to areas clearly defined for it by law. It should cooperate and collaborate with its sister security agencies in areas of mutual interests and in the national interest: gathering and sharing intelligence, information and tactics to help filter out undesirable political actors who have criminal records or who are facing terrorism, corruption or other criminal charges so that they can be excluded from the electoral process in line with the country's constitutional provisions, the extant laws of Nigeria and the law establishing the agency. Finally, it should be noted that a security apparatus that gets itself enmeshed recklessness in partisan politics loses its social credit and is atrophied. When it is able to avoid this, it would maintain its relevance, retain its credibility, restore its respect, enhance its dignity and reclaim its acclaim.

The performance of the EFCC as seen from the research context

A close and thorough examination and scrutiny of the scientific literature and other publications yielded the following thirteen (13) EFCC Appraisal Factors or Indicators which we shall identify and call in the study the EFCC APPRAISAL INDICES. They are:

(1)   Due Process Compliance
(2)   Human Rights Compliance
(3)   Inter-agency Cooperation
(4)   International Image
(5)   Leadership Image
(6)   Media Perception
(7)   Political Posture
(8)   Pro-active Enforcement
(9)   Public Acceptance
(10) Public Perception
(11) Public Relations
(12) Re-active Enforcement
(13) Enforcement Result/Outcome

When these identified factors were used to appraise the performance of the EFCC based on the literature parameters (readings of the literature and publications content analyzed) (see Borg and Gall's, 1989:114 recommendation), the following were the result on the performance of the EFCC on the above indicators/factors (see Table 12):

(1)   Due Process Compliance (Negative: –)
(2)   Human Rights Compliance (Negative: –)

(3)   Inter-agency Cooperation (Mixed: ±)

(4)   International Image (Positive: +)

(5)   Leadership Image (Mixed: ±)

(6)   Media Perception (Positive: +)

(7)   Political Posture (Negative: −)

(8)   Pro-active Enforcement (Negative: −)

(9)   Public Acceptance (Mixed: ±)

(10)   Public Perception (Mixed: ±)

(11)   Public Relations (Mixed: ±)

(12)   Re-active Enforcement (Mixed: ±)

(13)   Enforcement Result/Outcome (Mixed: ±)

Overall, the EFCC performance rating was mixed: 7 Mixed ratings; 4 Negative ratings; and 2 Positive ratings. The agency had positive ratings in International Image and Media Perception but poor (negative) ratings in Due Process Compliance, Human Rights Compliance, Proactive Enforcement and Political Posture (Politicization). It received Mixed ratings in Leadership Image, Inter-agency Cooperation, Public Perception, Public Relations, Re-active Enforcement and Enforcement Result/Outcome (see Table 12).

Based on these indicators, there is the need, therefore, for the agency to urgently work on almost all the identified areas, especially in the areas where the agency had Mixed/Negative ratings in order for it to perform its work better on all parameters to realize its objectives.

A thorough reading, content and documentary analysis of how the EFCC appears to be seen, viewed or perceived to have performed in twenty-three functional areas (EFCC MANDATE-FUNCTION: Table 13) in the literature and other publications (see chapter 2) on the agency is revealing. Facts gleaned from these sources and attendant findings on the functional performance of the EFCC in 23 main functional areas, shows that the overall performance rating of the agency was mixed. Based on EFCC mandate-functions identified in Table 13, the performance rating of the EFCC in 21 mandate-functions was mixed; two mandate-functions were rated negative; and no mandate-function was rated positive in EFCC performance.

Negative performance rating was received for the EFCC in the mandate-function area number 10: which deals with "matters connected with extradition, deportation and mutual legal or other assistance between Nigeria and any other country involving economic and financial crimes"; and in the mandate-function area number 17 which deals with the investigation of: "properties of any person if it appears to the Commission that the persons' lifestyle and extent of the properties are not justified by his source of income".

It appears certain from this, therefore, that the EFCC has fallen short of expectation in its functional performance. The agency would, therefore, need to improve its performance in all functional areas to realize its mandates and objectives.

When the EFCC Performance Appraisal Index Scorecard (Table 12) and EFCC Performance Appraisal Mandate-Specific Scorecard (Table 13) are juxtaposed, compared and combined, the same general picture emerges: On most of the parameters, the EFCC had a mixed rating in terms of general functional performance.

The findings find support in a survey poll conducted on the performance of the EFCC and ICPC in 2005. In the poll, Nigerians rated as "average" the efforts of the two agencies in their anti-graft and anti-corruption mandates. The poll, which was conducted, in the six geo-political zones, Lagos and Abuja asked respondents to indicate what they think about the performance of the agencies in the fight to stem the graft and corruption phenomenon. A breakdown of the total of 1601 respondents who responded shows the following:

Table 11: *Record Average Performance of EFCC and ICPC (2005)*

S/N	Survey Respondents	Nature of Response	Percentage of Response
1.	363	Great Extent	13.6%
2.	1422	Moderate Extent	52.8%
3.	602	Not At All	22.4%
4.	214	Not Sure	8.0%
Total	1601		100%

Source: "EFCC, ICPC Record Average Performance, says Poll" (2005:13). *The Guardian.* April 7.

The organization is a little less than 10 years in existence. It is still, relatively speaking, still in its infancy and developmental stages: These identified teething problems have vitiated its ability to perform to it optimal level to enable it achieve its objectives. The agency would, therefore, have to work hard on the identified parameters in the coming years to overcome those factors impeding its performance.

From all the foregoing, the overall appraisal of the performance of the EFCC can be summarized as follows:

(a)   In the eyes or perception of the EFCC and some individual observers, the agency has performed creditably well.

(b)   From the analysis of the various writings, publications, works and commentaries on the EFCC, the agency has fallen short of expectations: the EFCC has not performed well enough to be able to achieve its objectives.

(c)   From documentary analysis and interpretations of the literature based on the EFCC's mandate-specific functions, the agency functional performance have been a mixed bag.

(d)   On balance, the EFCC performance has been a mixed grill. The perceived factors impeding its performance need to be worked at if the agency is to be successful in realizing its mandate.

(e)   The perceived weaknesses and constraints are pointers to the fact that the agency still has a long trek to go before it can become an efficient, effective, pro-active, goal-oriented, goal-getting and highly performing law enforcement agency envisaged by its initiators/ creators and given birth to by the enabling EFCC (Establishment) Act 2004. In sum, it is still morning yet for the EFCC.

The former Chairman of the EFCC (Mrs. F. Waziri), seem to give veracity to this appraisal of her organization when she said:

> A lot of grounds have been covered in the last few years... The challenge, in my candid assessment, is to deepen current initiatives and consolidate the achievements of the recent past to guarantee their sustainability (Farida, 2011:7).

As recently as December 12, 2011, the new Acting Chairman of the EFCC (I. Lamorde) gave a verdict on the agency. He said: "For us to really move forward, the commission needs internal cleansing. Things have really gone wrong". To this, the Chairman of the Senate Committee on Drugs, Narcotics and Financial Crimes observed that anybody who has followed the establishment of EFCC will know that things have not been the same. He concluded "your (EFCC) credibility ratings have fallen" (EFCC staff, 2011:3).

A final note is in order here: The methodological approach and form of analysis employed here is invented, innovative and novel; and is dictated by the special circumstance of the study: the EFCC. Innovation, creativity, methodicality and novelty in any systematic enquiry are the essence of the scholarly enterprise. As a writer earlier succinctly puts it:

> The criticism of the EFCC… need not be waved aside, but studied… The most relevant question is: How should the EFCC be studied or investigated and analyzed? This is both a simple and at the same time a very complex question. It is simple in the sense that it is posed in such a way as to ordinarily elicit an instant, mechanically determined answer. Critically viewed, it is rather complex and its complexity is most likely attributed to the nature of the Nigerian society, and more technically, "the nature of the subject matter"… There is analytically speaking, a spate of theoretical (and methodological) confusion with respect to what the EFCC is, and how it goes about performing its mandate… The form of chosen analysis makes available some basic concepts, which are indispensable to a thorough, scientific research… The purpose of analysis especially in trying to expose all the minute properties that are to be explained is to make for a holistic understanding… For any theoretical/conceptual

formulation to be able to serve the purpose of the analysis of socially determined events, it must, as a condition, be suitable to what it hopes to explain... Intellectual discourse is relevant to the extent to which it is comprehensive... (comprehensible, scientific, methodical and utilitarian) ... This is the essence of scholarship. (Salami, 2007:108-122).

Table 12: *Functional Performance Appraisal Scorecard Rating of EFCC Based on Literature Findings (EFCC Appraisal Index)*

S/No	EFCC Appraisal Index	Rating	Rating Score
1.	Due Process Compliance	Negative	−
2.	Human Rights Compliance	Negative	−
3.	International Image	Positive	+
4.	Leadership Image	Mixed	±
5.	Inter-agency Cooperation	Mixed	±
6.	Pro-active Enforcement	Negative	−
7.	Media Perception	Positive	+
8.	Public Acceptance	Mixed	±
9.	Public Perception	Mixed	±
10.	Public Relations	Mixed	±
11.	Political Posture	Negative	−
12.	Re-active Enforcement	Mixed	±
13.	Enforcement Result/Outcome	Mixed	±

Appraisal Indicators/Indexes and attendant rating of performance of EFCC was obtained and isolated from extensive documentary analysis and scrutiny of the available literature and publications on the agency (see Chapters 2 and

3 for details of the Literature Review and the Research Methodology, respectively).

Table 13: *Functional Performance Appraisal Scorecard Rating of EFCC Based on Enabling Act Mandate – Specific Functions and Literature Findings*

S/No	EFCC Mandated Functions	Rating	Rating Score
1.	The EFCC is the designated Financial Intelligence Unit (FIU) in Nigeria which is charged with the responsibility of coordinating the various institutions involved in the fight against money laundering and enforcement of all laws dealing with economic and financial crimes in Nigeria.	Mixed	±
2.	The enforcement and administration of the provisions of the EFCC Act; and the coordination and enforcement of all economic and financial crime laws and enforcement functions conferred on any other person or authority.	Mixed	±
3.	Enforcement and due administration of the provisions of this Act.	Mixed	±

4.	Investigation of all financial crimes such as *Advanced Fee Fraud (otherwise known as 419), money laundering, counterfeiting, illegal charge transfers, futures market fraud, fraudulent encashment of negotiable instruments or fraudulent diversion of funds, computer credit card fraud, contract scam, forgery of financial instruments, issuance of dud cheques, etc.*	Mixed	±
5.	Adoption of measures to identify, trace, freeze, confiscate, or seize proceeds derived from terrorist activities, economic and financial crimes related offences, or the properties, the value of which correspond to such proceeds.	Mixed	±
6.	Adoption of measures to eradicate and prevent the commission of economic and financial crimes with a view to identifying individuals, corporate bodies or groups involved.	Mixed	±
7.	Facilitation and rapid exchange of scientific and technical information geared towards the eradication of economic and financial crimes.	Mixed	±

8.	Determination of the extent of financial loss and such other losses by government, private individuals or organizations.	Mixed	±
9.	Collaboration with government bodies within and outside Nigeria carrying out the functions wholly or in part analogous with those of the Commission.	Mixed	±
10.	Dealing with matters connected with extradition, deportation and mutual legal or other assistance between Nigeria and any other country involving economic and financial crimes.	Negative	–
11.	The collection of all reports relating to suspicious financial transactions, analyze and disseminate to all relevant government agencies.	Mixed	±
12.	Maintaining liaison with office of the Attorney General of the Federation, Nigerian Customs Service, Immigration and Prison Service Board, Central Bank of Nigeria, Nigerian Deposit Insurance Corporation, National Drug Law Enforcement Agency (NDLEA); all government	Mixed	±

	security and law enforcement agencies and such other financial supervisory institutions, in the eradication of economic and financial crimes.		
13.	Carrying out and sustaining rigorous public enlightenment campaign against economic and financial crimes within and outside Nigeria.	Mixed	±
14.	Any other such activities as are necessary to give effects to the functions conferred on the Commission under the Act.	Mixed	±
The Commission also has the power to:			
15.	Cause investigation to be conducted as to whether any body has committed an offence under this Act.	Mixed	±
16.	It can also investigate whether anyone is in the process of committing offences under the Act.	Mixed	±
17.	Investigate the properties of any person if it appears to the Commission that the persons lifestyle and extent of the properties are not justified by his source of income.	Negative	–

The Commission is also charged with the responsibility of enforcing the provisions of the following laws:			
18.	Money Laundering Amendment Act 2003, No. 7 1995, No. 13.	Mixed	±
19.	The Advance Fee Fraud and Other Related Offences Act 1995 as amended.	Mixed	±
20.	The Failed Banks (Recovery of Debts) and Financial Malpractices in Banks Act 1994 as amended.	Mixed	±
21.	The Banks and Other Financial Institutions Act, 1991 as amended.	Mixed	±
22.	Miscellaneous Offences Act (Cap. 410 LFN)	Mixed	±
23.	Any other law or regulations relating to economic and financial crimes, including the criminal code and penal code.	Mixed	±

Source: Functions of the EFCC are specified in Sections 1, 6 and 7 of the EFCC (Establishment Act 2004; and *Information Handbook 1:* EFCC (2004). Abuja: Mednat Ltd Production (pages 2 to 6). Ranking of Functional Performance of EFCC was obtained from extensive documentary analysis and scrutiny of the available literature and publications on the agency (see Chapters 2 and 3 for details of the literature review and the research methodology, respectively).

The performance of the EFCC as seen in a conclusive context

From all the foregoing multiple appraisals of the performance of the EFCC, the overall conclusion that one can arrive at is that the performance of the agency has been halting and mixed, but with an overwhelming or preponderance of the evidence weighing clearly to the verdict that the agency has performed less than expected. The net implication of this is that the EFCC has, in large measures, been unable to realize its mandates.

Indeed, to underscore the point, in a survey titled "How Would You Rate the EFCC at Eight" conducted from June 15, 2011 to June 24, 2011, twenty two of twenty three respondents (96% to 4%) rated the performance of the EFCC in eight years of its existence as poor. The majority of the respondents believed the agency has not achieved much in the last eight years; rather, they rated the performance of the agency as "ineffective", "biased", "selective", and "corrupt". The overall assessment was that the agency performed "below expectation" and the agency was "not worth a penny" (Adeoye and Ezeamalu, 2011). The same point was succinctly articulated on June 20, 2011 by Gabriel when he wrote:

> Stealing has become a major hobby and pastime for Nigerians in high places. It has even become a big time business... Nigeria's finances are milked, pillaged and bled everyday by the few who are privileged in the society. This is what the Economic and Financial Crimes Commission was set up to checkmate. So far, the body cannot boast that it has done it successfully (Gabriel, 2011).

For the EFCC to be able to perform optimally to achieve its objectives, therefore, a battery of measures are proffered and emplaced (Chapter 6) for effectuation to stem, address and indeed redress the constraints and factors which have vitiated and impeded the agency's performance in order to justify its establishment as an anti-graft and ant-corruption organization in the Nigerian polity. In sum, it can be said that it is still morning yet for the EFCC.

In the words of the former Chairman of the EFCC, Mrs. F. Waziri: "The challenge, in my candid assessment, is to deepen current initiative and consolidate the achievement of the recent past to guarantee their sustainability" (Waziri, 2011:7). To this, her predecessor in office added aptly: "Societies that have been able to move ahead are those that put the Statutes in place to criminalize corruption and ensure that the enforcement mechanisms are proper and ready for action" (Ribadu, 2009:1).

The founder and initiator of the EFCC, Chief Olusegun Obasanjo, perhaps, best sums up the matter when he categorically said that sadly government was not fighting corruption in Nigeria (Government Not, 2011:2). This point was further underscored in July, 2011 when the Attorney General and Minister of Justice of Nigeria called for the merger of the EFCC and the ICPC, saying that, as presently constituted, both agencies have not been able to realize the reasons for which they were created: to fight and stem economic and financial crimes and corruption [Nigeria: EFCC, ICPC, 2011].

Indeed, the EFCC has often been accused of paying lip-service to the anti-corruption war and of having a penchant for losing most of its high profile cases in court; of "incompetence"; being a "drain on the public purse"; unserious anti-graft agency; lacking zeal to fight corruption; complicit in perpetuating corruption; inefficient and unviable institution; dismissive of (the accused person's) rights to a speedy trial" and for being inept in the performance of its duties. All these, argues Emine (2012:4), cast big slurs on the fight against corruption in the country. This point was forceful made in April 23, 2012, when he noted:

> Generally, Nigerians are beginning to lose interest in the activities of the anti-graft agenc(y) (Emine, 2012:17).

Indeed, a most damning editorial/opinion in *The Nation* of April 11, 2012 at page 20 concluded that the EFCC has been a "BLOODY TOOTHLESS DOG!" in the face of the monumental level of thievery and corruption going on in Nigeria under its watch (see Cartoons H, I and J below).

Cartoon H: EFCC As A Bloody Toothless Dog!

Source: The Nation, April 11, 2012: 20.

Cartoon I: EFCC Before and Now

Source: Daily Sun. November 19, 2012:21.

Cartoon J: EFCC Blunted by Corruption

Source: Daily Sun (2012:21). December 5.

Incidentally, the United States-based Human Rights Watch, in a report released in August 2011 came to the same conclusion on the EFCC's performance. It said the Commission has only managed *four* convictions since it was established in December 2002 with the convicts spending little or no time in prisons (EFCC's successful convictions: Cecilia Ibru: 6 months; Tafa Balogun: 6 months; Diepreye Alamieyeseigha: 2 years; and Bode George: 2 years). The Report concluded:

> Other senior political figures who have been widely implicated (unresolved cases: Joshua Dariye, Abdullahi Adamu, Aliyu Akwe Doma, Saminu Turaki, Chimaroke Nnamani, Sam Egwu, etc) in corruption have not been prosecuted. Despite its promise; the EFCC has fallen far short of its potential and eight years after its inception, it left with a battered reputation and an uncertain record of accomplishment (EFCC: A fading, 2012: 23, 67).

In a damning summary of the performance of the EFCC from 2008 to 2013 with regards to seized assets in July 22, 2013, the editorial of the *Daily Sun* stated:

> The House of Representatives has resolved to investigate the status of assets seized by the Economic and Financial Crimes Commission (EFCC) from convicted criminals since its inception. Speaker Aminu Waziri Tambuwal revealed the House decision while declaring open a three-day public investigative hearing organised by its Committee on Drugs, Narcotics and Financial Crimes. ...

> According to him, "EFCC has between 2003 and now confiscated over 200 mansions and large sums of money

through 46 forfeiture court orders. These landed property, monies, and business concerns which were estimated to the worth in excess of ₦2 trillion, included bank accounts, shares in blue chip companies, exotic vehicles, fuel stations, holdings, warehouses and shopping malls." ...

We find it deplorable and disappointing that EFCC appears to be taking on the garb of a menace it was created to destroy. Recent reports on the finding of $170 million in an unidentified account, 200 seized houses which statuses are unidentified and 400 forfeited vehicles in different states of disrepair is, to say the least, appalling. It reeks of rancid indiscipline on the part of the EFCC that the agency that was set up to prevent theft and prosecute corrupt persons and organizations is now being forced to account for seized assets. That the commission came to this pass where it handling of seized assets is shrouded in secrecy is suspicious. That ₦2 trillion, which is almost 50 percent of Nigeria's total annual budget, has yet to be accounted for calls to question the integrity of the anti-graft agency. ...

The time has come for more light to be thrown on the activities of EFCC. (EFCC and the ₦2 trillion, 2013:19).

Writing on the same issue, *The Nation* in its editorial noted that: "it is a case of loot recovered simply to be re-looted" (Looting, 2013:19).

Finally, a commentator recently called the EFCC a "hopeless" agency that has rendered "mediocre performance" because of its "appaling" and "poor" achievement record. He concluded:

The EFCC's anti-corruption campaign is fast losing energy, concentration and public support. The achievement record of the agency has not given the public the confidence that the EFCC is moving in the right direction... An anti-corruption agency of government that looks the other way whenever senior government officers, politicians and business people are accused of corruption is not a fit and proper agency to investigate cases of corruption. This is why the public no longer pays heed to the anti-corruption catchphrase of the EFCC (Obijiofor, 2012:56).

In sum, another observer said the EFCC was "something of a *gra-gra* agency – a body that is peopled with exuberant officers eager to arrest suspects in order to hit the headlines" (Ribadu, 2013:21).

Chapter 6

Summary, Findings, Conclusions and Recommendations

Summary

The EFCC is a very important state institution in Nigeria which was created some 10 years ago (2002) but officially began its operations on April 16, 2003 to help government fight and stem the menace of economic and financial crimes which had plagued the country for years, corrupted the people, damaged the image of the country and stymied and stunted national development, growth and progress.

Despite the importance of this state institution, not much efforts have been made by researchers to undertake an in-depth scientific study of the agency or has serious attempts been made to assess, evaluate, appraise the organization as a whole or to put a searchlight on its performance or role in the Nigerian polity. This was the aim of this research.

In specific terms, the research discussed the historical background, philosophy, legal status and organizational structure which lie behind the development of the EFCC. The scientific literature concerning the agency, few as they are, were also reviewed. The study also explored in detail the performance of the agency since inception highlighting achievements, problems, challenges and constraints which have impeded and vitiated the performance of the agency. Solutions and recommendations to stem the challenges, constraints and problems were also proffered to improve the agency's performance and facilitate the realization of its mandate.

In general terms, the research was designed in part, to contribute to the knowledge and understanding of the role of the agency, to redress the void or gap created by the lack of scholarly research work in the subject area, and to appraise the performance of the organization from the date of its creation to-date (2002 to 2012) to see whether and how far it had been able to accomplish the objectives for which the agency was established by government about a 10 years ago.

Findings

The study identified those areas where the EFCC had performed well, those areas it needed to improve on and those areas it needed to change to make the agency effective and efficient in order to be able to deliver its mandate and onerous responsibilities to the country.

In general, the research found a mixed result on the performance of the EFCC: While the organization performed well in some areas to merit its establishment, in many other areas, the performance of the agency had been dismal and unimpressive.

In specific terms, the research found:

(a)   There was an embarrassing paucity of published and scholarly research works on the EFCC; and none done on the appraisal of the performance of such an important organization.

(b)   More than ever before, the study demonstrated that there was a pressing need to scientifically document the activities of the EFCC because it offers interesting research possibilities: The agency is still in a very active stage of transition and development. This process of change is important for the study of the administration of justice. To be able to document the transitional and developmental concepts of the EFCC will continue to be of inestimable value.

(c) The establishment of the EFCC had to some extent helped to restore Nigeria's tainted image in the international community and had helped to put in check, to some extent, the involvement of Nigerians in economic and financial crimes. The creation of the EFCC had helped to curtail, stem and reduce the incidence of the malfeasance in the country and launder the country's image.

(d) Government interference, politics, funding, leadership problems, duplication of functions, political abuse and misuse, use of police personnel, leadership recruitment restriction, inadequate infrastructure/education/ training facilities and opportunities, extra-judicial involvements, excessive turnover of headship and personnel, leadership immaturity and garrulousity, manpower shortages, over-stretching of personnel and facilities, non-presence in the vast area of the country, undue involvement in matters outside its jurisdiction and purview, violation of fundamental human and people's rights, undue delay in prosecution of cases; involvement in reactive rather than proactive enforcement, prolonged detention of suspects, excessive workload (over 200 petitions daily), conflicting/roles and uncooperative posture between EFCC and related-agencies, unhealthy rivalry, conflict and competition between EFCC and

155

fellow agencies, inadequate communication equipments, EFCC corruption, complicity and collusion with criminal elements, bias and partiality in investigations, arrests and prosecution, abuse of plea-bargaining, political persecution of ruling government opponents, over-exposure of EFCC personnel to politics and political roles, illegal and unlawful detentions, lack of political will by government, non-partnering with relevant security agencies and stakeholders, public apathy and uncooperativeness, selective trial, etc, have all combined to make the EFCC to not perform optimally to achieve its objectives and realize its mandate.

(e)   The EFCC was a political creation and continues to pursue political aims as dictated by the ruling political government. Till date, the politicization is pervasive. The net-result is that the agency has lost public confidence in the ability of the agency to perform and to be impartial.

(f)   The Act establishing the EFCC had constituted impediments to the smooth, efficient and effective operation of the organizations and has stifled the agency's performance. Some portions or sections of the Act would have to be amended to give the agency more bite.

(g)   The creation of the EFCC was to satisfy international interests and placate domestic needs/interests. There is the urgent need for reforms in the agency to enable it fight or stem economic and financial crimes.

(h)   Government efforts to fight graft has been half-hearted. An appraisal of the performance of the EFCC revealed a mix-grill. While the agency had made progress in some areas, it had also largely not been able to make progress in many areas relating to its mandate. The EFCC is now a shadow of itself (Ojo, undated).

Final verdict: Graft has continued to rise in Nigeria with Nigeria still listed among the most corrupt nations of the world by Transparency International and other agencies, despite the creation of EFCC (Eya, 2011:64). (See Table 9). In sum, the Attorney General of Nigeria indicted the EFCC and ICPC in 2011 for lacking "the capacity to conduct comprehensive investigations on fraudulent activities" and for lacking "the professional expertise to conduct investigations" (Nigeria: EFCC, 2011).

Conclusion

Arising from the findings of this research work, the following categorical conclusions can be made: the appraisal of the EFCC in Nigeria shows that the challenges before the agency to sanitize the polity in the areas of financial and economic crimes have been enormous, difficult and largely unrealized. The rather dismal performances of the EFCC have been predicated and underscored by a number of factors centring around the following areas:

(a)   In spite of the establishment of the EFCC, Nigeria over the years has lost over $400 billion to corruption perpetrated by its public officers. This situation has not abated rather it has been exacerbated (Ribadu's Dismissal, 2009:22).

(b)   The war against the hydra-headed monster of graft and corruption that has brought a potential nation, Nigeria, down on its knees is well, alive and thriving (Aiming, 2008:38).

(c)   Lack of political will by government to fight the malfeasance, interference in the affairs of the EFCC, gross inefficiency and ineffectiveness of the agency have contributed to the poor performance of the anti-graft agency.

We cannot do better to end this discussion of the appraisal of the EFCC, therefore, than to tap on the observations and views of some informed experts and scholars to lend credence to the research findings and conclusions; and indeed to buttress our concluding assertions. In this regard, the *Editorial of The Daily Sun* of May 24, 2011 at page 18 provides, like the other views after it, objective, independent and thorough *appraisal of the performance of the* EFCC when it tendered and rendered that:

> The recent report that Nigeria is among the top most corrupt countries in the world by the Berlin-based anti-graft organization, Transparency International speaks volumes of the incalculable damage corruption has done to the nation's image and the development of the country. It is disconcerting, indeed, that corruption among politicians and other public officials is increasing each year... Many of these crimes border on economic and financial heist and murders. Reining in the offenders has been an arduous task for the Economic and Financial Crimes Commission (EFCC). Many believe, rightly or wrongly, that the anti-graft agency has slowed down in sustaining the anti-corruption war... In some instances,

the anti-graft agency has been accused of treating cases preferred against high-profile politicians with kid gloves, and sometimes, strangely, drop the charges using the legalese of *nolle prosequi*... The challenge before the EFCC to sanitize the polity is enormous and so is public expectations (EFCC and Corruption, 2011:18).

Equally instructive is the view of the pioneer Chairman of the EFCC itself. He said:

I have always held the belief that the laws needed to check these problems often already exist; what is lacking is the culture of enforcement. Enforcement blossoms only where there is the necessary political will, and this political will must be strong at the very top. There is no place in the world where anti-corruption efforts will succeed without this political will, without leadership to promote the effort openly as a moral and political force. Without this will, the pressure on enforcement agents smothers their efforts and is destined to destroy the very agencies defined to lead the war against graft (Ribadu, 2009:155).

A final thought and damning verdict is provided by a scholar:

On paper, the agency is supposedly free to trail and give grief to corrupt officials. In reality, everybody knows that the anti-corruption agency often waits to receive clearance from the Presidency before summoning certain connected suspects for questioning. And even after the EFCC has received a nod to proceed, the President – or the nation's attorney-general or some other discerner of the President's mood – often sends signals about whether the EFCC should do a serious job of interrogation and prosecuting a suspect, or carry out a merely cosmetic feigned effort calculated to hoodwink. And woe-be-tide the anti-corruption crusader who ignores these Presidential cues... That strikes me as illustrating the pitfalls of combating corruption in Nigeria. The would-be anti-corruption agent first has to contend with a state whose impulse is to protect the most corrupt elements in order not to jeopardize the gargantuan, highly profitable corruption industry... (The President) may maintain the fiction that the EFCC is independent, absolutely immune from presidential meddlesomeness. That nostrum would only impress those who don't know that Nigeria is a nation where the EFCC and many other critical institutions are terribly weak, bereft of the kind of muscle, initiative and tradition that create and sustain independence... (The President needs to show) that under his watch, the fight against corruption will no longer be part deception, and part distraction (Ndibe, 2011:55).

Speaking at a book launch on June 14, 2011 at Abuja, the former Chairman and Chief Executive of the EFCC (Mrs. F. Waziri), in a sober reflection, said: "Today, Nigeria is devastated by a similar spell. For almost the whole of its life as a country, Nigeria has advertently lived with a self-imposed Sphinx known as corruption" (EFCC Not, 2011:4). Indeed, on November 22, 2012, the Chairperson of the EFCC (Ibrahim Lamorde) admitted before a Senate Committee on Drugs, Narcotics and Financial Crimes that the agency has largely failed in its mission: that the EFCC had failed over the years to nail high profile corrupt politicians, senior public servants, businessmen and women, and other crooked members of civil society (Obijiofor, 2012:56).

Unfortunately, the bitter truth is that the country's corruption profile is worse off today than it was at independence in 1960. In 2012, Nigeria is still heavily mired in the graft and corruption quagmire, murk, mirk or cul-de-sac with no respite in sight and no respite in the horizon. Summarizing this lamentable situation, Abbas (2010), said:

> For almost the whole length of her life as a country, Nigeria had advertently lived with a self imposed sphinx without any serious attempt to eliminate it... Corruption is Nigeria's own sphinx today. This sphinx has grown into such a monster that it is almost becoming impossible to conquer (Abbas, 2010).

The very last words on the performance of the EFCC from inception in 2002 to date (2012) is reserved for the United Nations analysts and a document published by Elombah titled "EFCC Report: No Difference between Ribadu and Waziri (2011), respectively.

A United Nations report in September 2011 on the situation states that Nigerians have lost faith in the EFCC, noting: "There isn't anything at all to indicate that (the Presidency) is willing to tackle corruption in a non-partisan manner". (Nigerians Have, 2011). To hammer home the point, the Elombah EFCC Report states:

> This report analyzes the most promising effort Nigeria's government has ever undertaken to fight corruption – the work of its Economic and Financial Crimes Commission (EFCC). Soon after it was established in December 2002, the EFCC began pursuing corruption cases in a way that publicly challenged the ironclad impunity enjoyed by Nigeria's political elite.
> Since its inception, the EFCC has arraigned 30 nationality prominent political figures on corruption charges and has recovered, according to the EFCC, some US$11 billion

through its efforts. But many of the corruption cases against the political elite have made little progress in the courts: there have been only four convictions to date and those convicted have faced relatively little or no prison time. Other senior political figures who have been widely implicated in corruption have not been prosecuted. At this writing, not a single politician was serving prison time for any of these alleged crimes. Despite its promise, the EFCC has fallen far short of its potential and eight years after its inception is left with a battered reputation and an uncertain record of accomplishment.

Most analysis of the EFCC has focused on the commission's two very different leaders. Nuhu Ribadu, the EFCC's first head, built the institution into what it is... (and) EFCC Chairman, Farida Waziri, who took over in 2008... But this report shows that in terms of tangible results, Waziri's record against high-level corruption is comparable to Ribadu's, and neither of them can claim much real success... Acts of spectacular incompetence have afflicted the EFCC under both Ribadu and Waziri (Elombah, 2011:2) (EFCC Report, 2011:1-3).

Adding to this, a writer concluded:

What would it take to rouse officials of the Economic and Financial Crimes Commission (EFCC) from snoozing while the nation is soaked in repugnant cases of corruption by parliamentarians, public office holders and celebrated businessmen and women? Ever since it was established ... the EFCC has pointed to its ambitious goals as an indication of its commitment to the fight against corruption. However, the EFCC's achievement record is poor... The extent to which the EFCC has lived by or adhered to its mission statement remains a contested topic in the public sphere. The EFCC has had a chequered history right from its early days. It is not a pretty history by anyone's evaluation... After many years of poor performance influenced by the self-serving interests and questionable integrity of the past and present President, the EFCC has never seen reason to be compelled to justify its existence. An anti-corruption agency that is funded and supported with tax payers' money must live up to public expectations and the key directives for which it was established (Obijiofor, 2012:19).

Recommendations

In the light of the summary, findings and conclusions made above, the following underlisted recommendations are proffered to address and redress the shortcomings and perceived flaws which have vitiated and impeded the ability of the EFCC to perform as a law enforcement agency. The intent is to foster and help move the agency forward, to be able to fight to stem economic and financial crimes and to enable it play its proper role in the Nigerian society in the most profound, professional, effective, efficient and robust way in order for it to realize its mandate and claim its proper place in the Nigerian clime. These batteries of recommendations can, additively and in combination, positively affect the fortune of the EFCC, burnish its image and brighten its future:

(1)   For the EFCC to function optimally without fear or favour, the agency must be independent of the Executive arm of government and be given a free hand to operate without undue government interference, hindrance and let.

(2)   To insulate the EFCC from politics and politicization, the appointment of its Chairman must be removed from

163

the President and placed in the National Assembly; same for members of the governing board of the commission. In addition, funds to run the agency should be derived from the Consolidated Revenue Fund of the Federation to ensure the agency's financial independence.

(3)   An efficient and effective EFCC would require for the agency to operate strictly within the mandate that was specified for it in the Act establishing it.

(4)   For an agency that is short-staffed, the EFCC is involved in too many cases spread over the whole country and abroad. The agency should, therefore, confine its activities to the most serious economic and financial crimes instead of dabbling into almost every conceivable criminal matters that are clearly outside its jurisdiction, power and mandate. Indeed, over the years, the agency has taken on almost every criminal and non-criminal matters outsides its purview, even taking over the functions of the ICPC and CCC. There is the urgent need, therefore, for the EFCC to restrict and confine or concentrate on serious crimes which have the potential of impacting most profoundly on national development, image, progress and morals: serious crimes of money-laundering, terrorism and high-level economic and financial crimes. The EFCC cannot afford to continue to be "Jack Of All Trades, Master Of None."

(5)   Indeed, the clear mandate for the establishment of the EFCC is the recovery of stolen public money and the prosecution of offenders and not on the prevention of corruption. To continue to dabble into the prevention of corruption is a clear deviation from its job description and mandate.

(6)   The EFCC must operate strictly as a professional outfit. It must not dabble into partisan politics or be involved in the electioneering process or be seen as a political tool of the government in power to haunt, harass and harangue political opponents and perceived enemies.

(7)   The EFCC should completely overhaul its apparatchik and streamline its operations so that it does not work at cross-purposes, as is currently the case, with other similar agencies such as the ICPC, Police and the CCC. Indeed, these agencies should work in tandem and complement one another in the fight against corruption and economic crimes.

(8)   To ensure that justice is speedily and quickly dispensed, and judgement rendered swiftly, the Act establishing the EFCC should be amended to facilitate the creation of a Special Court to hear and dispose of cases and so remove unnecessary legal technicalities that prolong unnecessarily the trial of offenders.

(9)   The Special Courts, which the *Daily Sun* indicated have been approved by the President of Nigeria and the Chief Justice of Nigeria, must be established speedily to clear the backlog of corruption cases in the regular courts (Special Courts, 2011:18).

(10)   The Special Financial and Economic Crimes Courts must and should be located in the 36-States of the country. The Courts would not only reduce the inordinate delays and abuses of the Court processes, it would also put the public on notice that the EFCC is serious about fighting corruption and graft.

(11) To enable the EFCC to perform optimally, the agency must establish offices in the 36 States of the country and in all the 774 local government council areas.

(12) To enhance EFCC prosecution of offenders, some aspects of the agency's enabling Act would have to be amended also especially in areas that border on abuse of preliminary objections, interlocutory application and deliberate delay of the judicial process.

(13) Alternatively, the 1999 Constitution should be amended to reduce delays in the trial of Court cases an area which the EFCC has identified as one of the banes against prosecution of offenders.

(14) For the EFCC to achieve its objectives, the agency must vigorously pursue and take seriously the issue of inter-agency cooperation, coordination and collaboration.

(15) The EFCC should continue to be given the powers to prosecute cases on their own with no recourse to the Attorney General who may, for political and other personal reasons, stall cases, refuse to prosecute offenders or shield suspects sent to him for political or other personal reasons.

(16) To increase EFCC personnel efficiency and effectiveness, the agency must severe ties and dependence on the police to execute its duties. It must be serviced wholly by its own staff. This requires for them to recruit and train their personnel. The Police has a poor image and corruption profile with the Nigerian public. The EFCC can do without this polluting and contaminating

influence. The EFCC, should as a matter of urgency, re-examine the process by which the staff of the agency are selected. As noted recently by a commentator: "The wholesale incorporation of police officers at top levels clearly affected the agency. Rather than creating a new force, it led to an adverse selection problem. The worst elements in the Nigeria Police infiltrated the organization carrying with them the same mindset for which the police was criticized" (Ugwuonye, 2011a:3). As another observer noted: The EFCC "is in the same boat with the Nigeria Police, whose rating has continually been on the downward trend" (Is EFCC, 2012:55).

Perhaps, the most damning assertion on the issue was recently offered by the Chairman, Senate Committee on Drugs, Narcotics and Financial Crimes. On August 5, 2013, he said:

I want to say that the problems with the anti-graft agencies are both institutional and operational.

It is institutional in the sense that the EFCC, as it is presently constituted is just like another arm of the Nigerian Police Force. Out of about one thousand, two hundred and fifty people (1,250), seven hundred (700) of them are policemen. This has dampened even the enthusiasm of the internation-al donor agencies because it is like funding another Nigerian Police Force. That has also slowed down rise of all the graduates that were employed and trained as Cadets. Besides, all the heads of departments in EFCC are policemen. This has also affected their 'promotion and affected employment opportunities. I believe that those are institutional problems that need to be tackled.

It is not only the police that have the rare knowledge of fighting corruption. There is no law that says it must be the police. Section 4 of the police act says that they are empowered to arrest, investigate and prosecute. You can have a few of them for the purposes of arrest, but to have 700 of them is definitely unacceptable. What that also means is that as it is now, the policemen take their pay from the police force and also take allowances from the EFCC. Such allowances that should have been used to employ people, you use them in giving people who are just out there on a jamboree. I think that is not right. … EFCC should be restructured (EFCC, another arm, 2013:24).

(17) The EFCC should establish a well-developed selection and recruitment process to help it filter out undesirable elements and attract into its rank and file individuals who are highly qualified, competent and credible.

(18) The EFCC needs to strengthen and deepen the quality and quantity of its personnel who are currently over-worked and over-stretched and spread too thin to make their impact felt across the length and breath of Nigeria and abroad. The EFCC is concentrated heavily in Abuja, Lagos, Port Harcourt, Enugu, Kano and Gombe but virtually absent in the other parts of the country.

(19) The EFCC is currently under-funded. Increased funding is needed from government. Both EFCC and government must be serious and not tackle the menace and graft half-heartedly to be able to attract funding from foreign donor countries and entities.

(20) The Freedom of Information Bill became law on May 27, 2011. The EFCC should avail itself of the passage not only to partner more with the public in the fight against graft and corruption but also to be more forthcoming and transparent with the public, the press and other stakeholders on its actions and activities.

(21) Apart from funding, the EFCC should also be properly furnished with state-of-the art, modern and scientific equipments communication and ICT facilities, vehicles and office spaces. In addition, the staff of the agency must be provided emoluments, incentives and promotion on a regular basis and also be well paid.

(22) On its part, the EFCC believes that its functional performance would be enhanced if there is a non-conviction based assets forfeiture law is emplaced; if out-dated laws are repealed and replaced by ones based on an appraisal of Nigeria's national realities and if some foreign countries cooperate with the agency in the retrieval of stolen funds in their countries (Waziri, 2011b).

(23) The EFCC should completely discard the alien, unlawful, imported and often abused concept of plea-bargain. Plea bargain does not exist under Nigerian laws; and in the interest of the nation and justice must be frowned at and jettisoned.

(24) The public generally perceives the EFCC as an agency that is politicized, that handles its work selectively to favour government officials and the ruling class to the detriment of political opponents and enemies. To remove and correct this perception, the EFCC must not

only be professionals in their duties, they must also launder their image by establishing complaints-handling machineries to resolve long-standing or perceived issues with the public. This they can do in three ways: (a) Whenever necessary, the EFCC should institute Internal Investigations on the conduct of its staff; (b) the agency should create EFCC Review Boards to investigate citizen complaints; and (c) the EFCC should establish an Ombudsman to investigate matters against it as an organization. Without public support and cooperation, the agency's ability to perform optimally would be a mirage.

(25) The Nigerian public must cooperate and support the EFCC for the agency to realize its mandate. The public must take the fight against graft and economic crimes as a collective endeavour and not as the exclusive preserve of the EFCC if the country is to have an effective handle on the phenomena.

(26) Some commentators have noted that the EFCC is the biggest threat to human rights in Nigeria; and that the agency poses danger to human rights more than any other law enforcement agency even during the military. Consequently, despite the popular indulgent attitude toward the agency, its future and ultimate relevance in Nigeria will depend on how it is measured relative to the degree to which EFCC's operations are to be consistent with the basic rights of the citizens. To this extent, the EFCC must be reformed to follow and respect human rights and due process in the performance of its mandate. (Ugwuonye, 2011a).

(27) The EFCC must be given enabling powers to fight graft and corruption at all levels of the Nigerian society. This would require that appropriate legislations and tools be put in place to grow the agency and make it an effective and efficient institution that is capable of discharging its responsibilities.

(28) The EFCC should be under the control of a supervisory authority. It should not operate as a super-agency independent of any controlling or supervisory government body. The 2004 Act which created the EFCC is not superior to the provisions of the Nigerian Constitution. Instructively, Chapter 1, Part 1, Section (1) of the 1999 Constitution categorical states: *"This Constitution is supreme and its provisions shall have binding force on all authorities and persons throughout the Federal Republic of Nigeria."* Section 174(i)(a) of the 1999 Constitution states that it is within the purview of the Office of the Attorney-General to supervise, if not control, the activities of all agencies like the EFCC in the country. Indeed, the authority of the Attorney General to have oversight on the EFCC, ICPC, and the Police cannot be in question. He is the Chief Law Officer of the Federation. To allow the EFCC to operate with reckless abandon as it has done in the past is a steady invitation to lawlessness and anarchy; and is a negation of the rule of law which is the plank upon which civilized conduct in government lies or is built.

(29) The provision that says the EFCC should be headed by a police officer not below the rank of Assistant Commissioner of Police is defective and should be amended. The tenure of the head of the agency should

171

be tenured and pegged at 5 years only. The appointment of the head should be terminal: upon the expiration of tenure, the head should not return to government bureaucracy; and therefore, while in office, should not be blinded by the illusion of a return to whatever he or she was seconded from. The appointment of the head of the agency should not be limited to service personal only. Indeed, men and women with integrity and requisite credential should be eligible to occupy the position (The Criteria, 2012:14).

(30) The removal from office of the first two Chairmen of the EFCC completely destabilized and slowed down the work of the agency. To fight the essential war on graft and corruption, therefore, the country and indeed the EFCC should endeavour to build systems that work and which transcend individuals. In this regard, the Editorial commentary of *The Nation* is instructive: "Individuals are important, but only contribute their quotas and leave the stage when necessary. It amounts to poverty of state that the business of state can only be done by an individual. Nobody should be indispensable". This is a lesson and a challenge to the EFCC (Ribadu's Course, 2008:13).

APPENDICES

Appendix 1

Farida Waziri (2008-2011)
her footprints, her legacy

Right from her first day in office, Mrs. Waziri knew she had to swim against the tide given the controversial manner in which her predecessor, indefatigable Mallam Nuhu Ribadu was eased out of office. In spite of the removal of the EFCC chairman, her tormenting tenure recorded some outstanding achievements which cannot be wished away. Irrespective of criticisms that Mrs. Waziri is a lame duck, she has scored many FIRSTS within three years. According to a document obtained by our correspondent a few highlights of her achievements are as follows:

- Secured over 400 convictions in the past three years. These represent about two-third of all convictions secured since the establishment of the Commission in 2003.

- Inherited about 10 high profile cases from her predecessor in 2008 but she has taken over 65 of such high profile cases to courts, with another 1,500 other cases pending in courts. Some of the several fresh high profile cases which include cases of former Governors, Ministers, bank chief executives, heads of parastatals and agencies. Some of these high profile cases include those of Michael Botmang, Boni Haruna, Rasheed Ladoja, Bode George, Femi Fani-Kayode, Babalola Borisade, Hassan Lawal, Cecilia Ibru, Erastus Akingbola, Sebastian Adigwe, Francis Atuche, Dimeji Bankole, Nasir El-Rufai, Otunba Adebayo Alao-Akala; Gbenga Daniel; Danjuma Goje; and Aliyu Akwe Doma.

- Made recoveries of over $9 billion USD in the last three years.

- Developed and deployed Eagle Claw software that is changing the face of fighting cyber crime and 419 in Nigeria. Project Eagle Claw is software that sniffs out all fraudulent e-mails and monitors them with the option of shutting down such mails. This means that all 419 e-mails emanating from Nigeria will either be monitored or be shut down. Over 5,000 fraudulent email addresses have so far been shut down and over 80 suspects already facing trial.

- Set up a Transactions Clearing Platform (TCP) which is help desk for foreign investors. This has saved thousands of prospective victims from the U.S and other parts of the world from falling victims.

- Initiated a special training for officers of the Commission and commenced Project Eagle-Eye which leads to tax investigations (amongst other issues) with a target of recoveries of ₦120 billion for the Federal Government of Nigeria annually.

- Instituted an aggressive programme of sensitisation of the public and whistle blowing to ensure their buy-in into the Anti-Corruption Revolution Campaign, (ANCOR).

- Championed the enactment of a non-conviction based assets forfeiture legislation to compliment the present conviction-based regime. The Bill is in the National Assembly for passage into law. This is in addition to championing the amendment of the Money Laundering Act which has been achieved.

- Initiated, with the Federal Ministry of Education, the process for the introduction of anti-corruption curriculum at all levels of education in Nigeria.

- Floated and got Federal Executive Council's approval for insurance scheme for staff and assets of the Commission with effect from February 2010.

- Completed a salary survey and made recommendation for a new pay structure for staff which has taken effect and aimed at insulating staff from external pressures and temptations.

- Initiated and commenced work on the permanent office complex of the EFCC sitting on 5.5 hectares of land along Airport Road, Abuja. Vice-President Namadi Sambo did the ground-laying ceremony of the complex recently and work is on-going on the office complex.

- Repositioned the Nigerian Financial Intelligence Unit to make it more proactive and responsive to strategic intelligence.

- Deployed the GoAML and GoCase softwares that were stagnated. This has thrown up a lot of high profile cases.

- Briefed Price Water House Coopers to do diagnostic review of the EFCC and recommend administrative structures that will guarantee a career path for officers and motivate them to ensure the realisation of EFCC's mandate.

- Set up the Monitoring and Intelligence Units. These units have ensured pro-active gathering of information to facilitate investigations even in the absence of petitions.

- Renegotiated the expired MoU with Microsoft to cover a wider spectrum of issues. The new MoU has since been signed.

- Leveraged on the fresh MoU and brought together a coalition of parties involving Microsoft, the African Development Bank, Western Union, Yahoo! Google, Coca-Cola, etc to support the fight against Internet Fraud. The first West African Summit hosted by this Coalition was held in 2010.

- EFCC's Training and Research Institute, TRI, has been tremendously transformed in terms of infrastructural development and curricular expansions in the last three years. The transformation of the TRI has made it the hub of FBI organised trainings for Nigerian law enforcement agencies.

Source: "For The Records" (2011:4). *Vanguard.* November 25.

Appendix 2

Farida Waziri Threatens to Expose Obasanjo's Corruption

My attention has been drawn to a number of allegations made against me by Mr Obasanjo. One of such was the alleged involvement of former Delta state governor, James Ibori in my appointment. While I hold the office of a Head of state, either serving or retired in the highest esteem, I will like to put on record for the umpteenth time that this is totally unfounded, blantant lie and arrant falsehood. It is therefore worrisome when a man who has been twice a Nigerian head of state can descend so low to peddle falsehood. The truth is that I never met Ibori in my life until after months in office as chairman of the EFCC when I used to see him in the presidential villa.

It is on record today that I initiated the investigation that drove Ibori into the waiting hands of Interpol and Metpolice. As such, it is illogical and nonsensical for anyone to continue to insinuate that Ibori has a hand in my appointment. I remember this was one of the lies Obasanjo's sit-tight pawns cooked to stop my appointment as EFCC chairman in 2008.

On the issue of qualifications raised by Obasanjo, the qualification for appointment as chairman of the Commission as stipulated in its Establishment Act says that the chairman shall 'be a serving or retired member of any government security or law enforcement agency not below the rank of Assistant Commissioner of Police or equivalent; and possess not less than 15 years cognate experience'. Late President Yar'Adua did not have to alter the Establishment Act when he was appointing me unlike what Obasanjo did.

Again for the records, I served in the Nigeria Police force for 35 years and got to the pinnacle of my career before my appointment as EFCC chairman. If Obasanjo's real age has not blurred his memory, I will like to remind him that I was a Commissioner of Police, Admin Force CID, CP General Investigations, CP Anti-fraud, CP X squad, CP Police Special Fraud Unit where I secured the first conviction in a case of Advance Fee Fraud in Nigerian history. These are all prime investigative organs of the Nigeria Police where I related with other law enforcement agencies including the FBI across the world. I must place on record that at SFU, I did not only relate with FBI, Interpol and Metpolice among others, we carried out joint operations at different times on a number of cases. I have also led the Nigerian delegation to the Interpol headquarters in France.

To further expose the height of mischief in the allegations, the past and present chairmen of the EFCC have both worked under me, yet someone can open his mouth to say I am not qualified to head the same agency. This is in addition to my educational qualifications such as a first degree in Law, a Master degree in Law and another Master degree in Strategic studies. I doubt if Obasanjo himself can boast of this level of educational qualifications.

I will also like to remind Obasanjo that no chairman of the EFCC has till date beaten my records in terms of investigation of high profile cases, prosecution, conviction and recovery.

I will like to warn that those who live in glass house don't throw stones and as such Obasanjo should not allow me open up on him. Respectable elder statesmen act and speak with decorum.

Signed:

Dr (Mrs) Farida Waziri, OFR
Former Chairman of the Economic and Financial
Crimes Commission, EFCC

*Source:*http://elombah.com/index.php/articles-mainmenu/17694-farida-waziri-threatens-to-expose-obasanjo-s-corruption: September 11, 2013.

Appendix 3

(How) Mrs Farida Waziri (Allegedly) tried to bribe Chief Olusegun Obasanjo to retain her job as EFCC Chairman

[elombah.com] Mrs Farida Waziri (allegedly) tried to bribe Chief Olusegun Obasanjo to retain her job as EFCC Chairman, but he (allegedly) refused her offer. The (purported) attached letter below (purportedly) made available to elombah.com clearly speaks for itself. Mrs Farida Waziri threatened to expose Obasanjo, but she (allegedly) ended up being exposed herself.

Elombah.com recalls that Mrs Farida Waziri, this week hit back at former President Olusegun Obasanjo over Mr. Obasanjo's criticism of her leadership at the EFCC.

The former EFCC boss accused Mr. Obasanjo of manipulating the EFCC under Nuhu Ribadu to hunt political opponents in Mr. Obasanjo's effort to secure a third term in office.

The former president had told a publication of the EFCC, Zero Tolerance, that Mrs. Waziri was a disaster to Nigeria's effort against corruption, questioning her qualification for the appointment in the first place, and accusing , Mrs Waziri of having been appointed on the recommendation of convicted former governor, Delta state, James Ibori.

Mr. Obasanjo said Mrs. Waziri, a retired police officer, who took over as chairperson of EFCC after the removal of Mr. Ribadu, did so much to reverse Mr. Ribadu's achievements in the war against corruption.

"I know that the woman they brought in to replace Ribadu (Farida Waziri) was not the right person for that job, because I understood that one of those who head-hunted her was James Ibori," Mr. Obasanjo had told the paper.

"If James Ibori, who is now in a U.K. prison for fraud, head-hunt somebody who will fight corruption in Nigeria, then you can understand what happened," he added.

When questioned further on his stance on the former anti-graft chief, Mr. Obasanjo said Mrs. Waziri was not adequately qualified to head the EFCC.

"Well, go and look at her track record," he said. "Go and look at the condition or the qualification; go and look at the type of interaction that anybody holding that job will have with a similar organisation elsewhere; did Waziri have that type."

"What connection did she have with FBI, what relationship did she have with Metropolitan Police in London. It's not a picnic," he added.

The (purported) letter above (allegedly) showed that Mrs Waziri begged Obasanjo to plead with Jonathan to reconfirm her for a second term and pledged to work for the interest of the former president with regards to Ogun State politics, but in a reaction on Wednesday, Mrs. Waziri warned Mr. Obasanjo to respect his age and watch his comments, and accused him of using Mr. Ribadu, who served under Mr. Obasanjo, to witch-hunt political opponents in a "rabid" pursuit of a third term.

"Former Chairman of the Economic and Financial Crimes Commission, EFCC, Dr (Mrs) Farida Waziri,OFR has reminded former President Olusegun Obasanjo that ability to be used to witch hunt political enemies in the rabid pursuit of a third term agenda has never been part of the qualifications for appointment as chairman of the anti-graft agency," Mrs. Waziri said in a statement on Wednesday.

Mrs. Waziri denied meeting Mr. Ibori ahead of her appointment to the EFCC, a claim she made earlier in a separate interview with the same EFCC publication. Mr. Ibori is serving a jail term in United Kingdom for stealing state funds.

The former EFCC boss said she was fully qualified to have headed to the agency given the stipulations of the law.

She said, "On the issue of qualifications raised by Obasanjo, the qualification for appointment as chairman of the Commission as stipulated in its Establishment Act says that the chairman shall 'be a serving or retired member of any government security or law enforcement agency not below the rank of Assistant Commissioner of Police or equivalent; and possess not less than 15 years cognate experience'. Late President Yar'adua did not have to alter the Establishment Act when he was appointing me unlike what Obasanjo did".

"Again for the records, I served in the Nigeria Police force for 35 years and got to the pinnacle of my career before my appointment as EFCC chairman. If Obasanjo's real age has not blurred his memory, I will like to remind him that I was a Commissioner of Police, Admin Force CID, CP General Investigations, CP Anti-fraud, CP X squad, CP Police Special Fraud Unit where I secured the first conviction in a case of Advance Fee Fraud in Nigerian history. These are all prime investigative organs of the Nigeria Police where I related with other law enforcement agencies including the FBI across the world. I must place on record that at SFU, I did not only relate with FBI, Interpol and Metpolice among others, we carried out joint operations at different times on a number of cases. I have also led the Nigerian delegation to the Interpol headquarters in France."

"To further expose the height of mischief in the allegations, the past and present chairmen of the EFCC have both worked under me, yet someone can open his mouth to say I am not qualified to head the same agency. This is in addition to my educational qualifications such as a first degree in Law, a Master degree in Law and another Master degree in Strategic studies. I doubt if Obasanjo himself can boast of this level of educational qualifications.

"I will like to warn that those who live in glass house don't throw stones and as such Obasanjo should not allow me open up on him. Respectable elder statesmen act and speak with decorum," she concluded.

Source: http://elombah.com/index.php/special-reports/17739-revealed-mrs-farida-waziri-tried-to-bribe-chief-olusegun-obasanjo-to-retain-her-job-as-efcc-chairman: Friday, 13 September 2013.

Bibliography

"A Case of Hunting the Hunter" (2010). *THISDAY*. March 23:25.

"A War Gone Comatose" (2008). *Tell*. December 1.

Abbas, Femi (2010). "EFCC and Nigeria's Own Sphinx". *Posted*. April 8.

Abubakar, Abdul-Rahman (2011). "Nigeria: EFCC, ICPC Lack Capacity to Investigate – Adoke." *Daily Trust*. July 1.

Adamu, Mohammed (2005). "AIT's For Political Witch-Hunt." *The Punch*. January 12.

Adebayo, Akeem (2009). "A Letter From Dublin to Sanusi Lamido." *The Guardian*. August 26.

Adeniyi, Olusegun (2011). *Power, Politics and Death*. Yaba, Lagos: Kachifo Limited.

Adeoye, Gbenro and Ben Ezeamalu (2011). "How Would You Rate the EFCC at Eight" (23 Responses). *Posted:* June 15.

Aderounmu, A. (2008). "Poor Man Wey Steal Magi Cube…!" *Posted:* October 28.

Aderounmu, A. (2009). "1960-2008: Nigeria has wasted 2 generations and 48 years." *Posted:* January 6.

Aderounmu, A. (2009). "Nigerian Judiciary, A Citadel of Corrupt Minds." *Posted:* December 18.

"AG vs EFCC: Aondoakaa's Move has Political Undertone – NBA, WABA, Others" (2007). *Vanguard.* September 21:43 – 46.

"Aiming For His Head" (2008). *Tell.* December 1.

Ajagun, S.O. (2009). An Evaluation of Some Selected Anti-Corruption Policies in Nigeria: A Case Study of Edo State, Nigeria. A Ph.D. Thesis submitted to the Department of Public Administration, Ambrose Alli University, Ekpoma, Edo State.

"Akingbola Urges Court to Stop EFCC From Arraigning Him" (2011). *The Nation.* May 24:3.

Akintunde, M. (1994). "Trouble in the Till". *Newswatch.* February 14.

Akpochafo, Peter (2011). "The Nigerian LNG Project Corruption Scandal — The EFCC And The Nigerian Individual Bribe Takers." *Posted:* April 15.

Allacess (2008). "Re: A Letter to Mrs. Farida Waziri, EFCC Chairman". *Posted:* July 29.

"Alleged ₦10 Billion Loan: Bankole Under House Arrest" (2011). *The Nation*. June 4.

"America's Support For Scrapping of EFCC Unlikely" (2012). *The Nation*. April 19.

Anderson, J., Durston, B. and Poole, M. (1970). *Thesis and Assignment Writing*. Brisbane: Wiley.

"Anti-Corruption War is on Course" (2008). *Tell*. December 1.

"Aondoakaa: The AGF on the Firing Line" (2007). *Vanguard*. September 21:42.

Aresa, F.M. (2011). "AGF, EFCC & ICPC See No Evil – Do No Evil – Loot No Evil."

Ariteni (2008). "Re: A Letter to Mrs. Farida Waziri, EFCC Chairman". *Posted:* July 29.

Arndt, Christiane & Charles Oman (2006). *Uses and Abuses of Governance Indicators*. Paris: OECD Development Centre.

Asemota, S.A. (2002). "The Imperative of National Security is Justice": Defence of Memorandum of CSMN." Benin City: Aiviz Robin Production.

"ASUU Kicks Again Plea Bargaining" (2012). *The Nation*. November 21.

Atojoko, S. (2003). "Rape of a Nation". *Newswatch*. February 24.

"Attorney-General In The Dock" (2009). *Tell*. September 28.

"Audu Sue EFCC For Declaring Him Wanted" (2006). *Vanguard*, October 10:1, 14.

Ayobolu, Jide (2006). "EFCC, Corruption And The Due Process." *Posted:* November 2.

Babafemi, Femi (2011). "EFCC's Mandate In Proper Perspective". *Sunday Sun.* October 23.

Babarinsa, D. (1996). "Return of the Bad Boys." *Tell.* February 12.

Bain, R. (1962). "The Most Important Sociologists?" *American Sociological Review*. Vol. 27. October (pages 746 – 748).

"Bankole Fault EFCC's Invitation Procedure" (2011). *The Nation.* June 2.

"Bankole's Father Cries Out, they want to kill my son" (2011). *Daily Sun.* June 14.

Bello-Imam, I.B. (2005). *The War Against Corruption in Nigeria: Problems and Prospects*. Ibadan: College Press & Publishers Limited.

Bertok, Janos & Elodie Beth (2005). *Public Sector Integrity: A Framework for Assessment*. Paris: OECD Development Centre.

Borg, W.R. and Gall, M.D. (1989). *Educational Research: An Introduction*. 5th Edition. New York: Longman.

Brew, A. (2001). *The Nature of Research: Inquiry in Academic Contexts*. London: Routledge.

Bruce, C.S. (1994). "Research Students' Early Experiences of the Dissertation Literature Review." *Studies in Higher Education*. Vol. 19. No. 2 (217 – 29).

Camerer, Marianne (2006). "Measuring Public Integrity". *Journal of Democracy*. Vol. 17. No. 1. (152-165).

CBN, NDIC Differ Over Fraud Cases in Banks (2003). *The Guardian*. September 2.

"Charges Against Bankole Nonsensical" (2011). *Daily Sun*. June 13.

"CJN Faults Plea Bargain, injunctions against arrest" (2011). *The Guardian*. November 16.

"Controversial Directive On EFCC" (2007). *Vanguard*. August 12:10.

Cooper, H.M. (1988). "The Structure of Knowledge Synthesis." *Knowledge in Society*. Vol. 1 (104 – 126).

"Corruption: Civil Society Groups Set Agenda For Jonathan" (2011). *Sunday Sun*. June 2.

"Dariye: The Final Rush" (2006). *Tell*: 27.

Duncan, Nick (2006). "The Non-Perception Based Measurement of Corruption: A Review of Issues and Methods from a Policy Perspective" in *Measuring Corruption*, Charles Sampford, Arthur Shacklock, Carmel Connors, & Fredrik Galtung (eds). Hampshire: England & Burlington, Vermont: Ashgate Publishing. (131-161).

Editorial/Opinion (2011). *The Nation*, October 10.

"EFCC: A fading toothless bull dog?" (2012). *The Nation*. April 29.

"EFCC and Corrupt Politicians" (2011). *Daily Sun.* May 24:18.

"EFCC and Nigeria Anti-Corruption War" (2008). (http://www.saharareporters. com/wazirijeepscandal.php).

"EFCC and the ₦2 trillion seized assets" (2013:19). *Daily Sun*, July 22.

"EFCC Arrest Ex-Kogi Governor" (2006). *The Punch*. November 30:9.

"EFCC Arrests Kalu, Turaki" (2007). *Vanguard*. July 12:1, 15.

"EFCC Before... Now" (2012:21). *Daily Sun*. November 19.

"EFCC Disagrees With Bola Ajibola On Plea Bargain" (2007). *Vanguard*. August 9:1, 15.

"EFCC Liaises With INEC Against Corrupt Governors, Others" (2006). *Vanguard*. December: 10.

"EFCC Minus Ribadu" (2007). *Vanguard*. July 19:31.

"EFCC Not Dramatising Trial of Suspects" (2011). *The Nation*. June 15.

"EFCC Now To Concentrate On Money Laundering, Terrorism" (2007). *Vanguard*. July 2:1, 15.

"EFCC Raises Alarm Over Campaign of Calumny" (2011). *Daily Sun*. June 1.

"EFCC Report: No Difference Between Ribadu and Waziri (2011) (elombahperspective@gmail.com).

"EFCC Staff to undergo lie detector test" (2011). *Daily Sun*. December 13.

"EFCC Unserious With Ex-Governor's Trial" (2008). *The Punch*. December 10:1-2.

"EFCC, ICPC, FRSC, 35 others to go" (2012). *Daily Sun*. April 17.

"EFCC, ICPC Record Average Performance, says Poll" (2005). *The Guardian*. April 7.

"EFCC, It is the Return of the Nigeria Police" (2007) *Vanguard*. February: 18.

"EFCC, Please Walk the Talk" (2011). *The Nation*. May 23:21.

"EFCC: Between Petition, Conviction" (2006). *Vanguard*. October 10:18.

"EFCC's Last Act" (2007). *Vanguard*. February 22:31.

"EFCC Makes Key Appointments" (2012). *Sunday Sun*. March 11.

Eke, C.E. (2006). "How Dare You Criticize Nigeria EFCC". Los Angeles, California. September 24.

Emine, George (2012). "EFCC: Paying Lip Service To Anti-Corruption War". *Nigerian Newsworld*. April 23.

Enweremadu, D.U. (2010). *Anti-Corruption Policies in Nigeria Under Obasanjo and Yar'Adua: What To Do After 2011?* Abuja: Friedrich Ebert Stiftung.

"Ex-Governors are Scapegoats" (2007). *Vanguard*. August 12:10.

"Ex-Speaker's Arrest Political" (2011). *Daily Sun*. June 15.

"Exit Waziri" (2011). *The Nation*. November 25.

Eya, W. (2011). "What Nigerians Expect From Jonathan". *Saturday Sun*. May 8.

"Farida — Nothing to applaud" (2011). *Vanguard*. November 25.

"From Arraigning Him" (2011). *The Nation*. May 24:3.

"From The Editor" (2008). *Tell*. June 2.

"From The Editor" (2009). *Tell*. September 28

"From The Editor" (2010). *Tell*. June 7.

Gabriel, Omoh (2011). "Stealing Nigeria Blind and Failure of EFCC to Stop the Thieves". *Finance*. June 20.

Galtung, Fredrik (2006). "Measuring the Immeasurable: Boundaries and Functions of (Macro) Corruption Indices", in *Measuring Corruption*, Charles Sampford,

Arthur Shacklock, Carmel Connors, & Fredrik Galtung (eds). Hampshire: England & Burlington, Vermont: Ashgate Publishing. (101-130).

"Government Action Waters Corruption" (2009). *Tell*. September 28.

"Government Not Fighting Corruption" (2011). *The Nation*. June 16.

"Governors on Their Knees" (2007). *Tell*, No. 22 May 28: 20.

"Graft: No Protection For My Sponsors – Yar'Adua" (2007). *Vanguard*. August 7.

"Hands Off Bankole" (2011). *Daily Sun*. May 30.

Haruna, M. (2011). "Between The Senate and the House Leadership". *The Nation*. June 15.

"How Yar'Adua Reversed Self On EFCC, ICPC, Conduct Tribunal – Presidency" (2007) *Vanguard*. August 12:11.

"Ibori, The EFCC and the Future of Nigeria's Anti-Corruption Crusade" (2007). *Posted:* December 18.

"Ibori: EFCC Adds More Charges" (2007). *Vanguard*. December, 19:10.

"Igbinedion Returns, Faces EFCC today as UN body writes Yar'Adua on Ribadu" (2008). *Vanguard*. January 21:1, 5.

Igbinovia, P.E. (1980). "The Police in Modern Nigeria". *Police Studies: International Review of Police Development*. Vol. 3. No. 3. Fall.

Igbinovia, P.E. (1984). "How International Are Criminal Justice Journals?: A Content Analysis of The International Functional Agenda of Two American Journals." International Journal of Comparative and Applied Criminal Justice. Vol. 8. No. 1. June.

Igbinovia, P.E. (2003). The Criminal in All of Us: Whose Ox Have We Not Taken? Inaugural Lecture Series No. 71. Benin: University of Benin Press.

"I know those after my job – Farida Waziri" (2011). *Daily Sun.* August 16.

Imam, I. and M.A. Mustapha (undated). "Combating Corruption in Nigeria: The Role of The Legislature Examined". Undated paper.

Information Handbook 1: EFCC (2004). Abuja: Mednat Ltd Production.

"Is EFCC Born Again?" (2012). *Sunday Sun.* April 1.

Jason, Pini (2011). "EFCC, Conjectures and the rule of law". *In Pini Jason.* July 9.

Jerryboy_2010@yahoo.co.uk (2010). "The Role of EFCC in Restoring Nigeria's Past Glory".

"Jonathan: New Era, Old Challenges" (2011). *The Nation.* May 6.

"Jonathan's Big Challenge" (2010). *Tell.* June 7.

"Jonathan Sacks EFCC Boss, Farida Waziri" (2011). *National Mirror.* November 24.

June, Raymond, Afroza Chowdhury, Nathaniel Heller, and Jonathan Werve (2008). *A Users' Guide to Measuring Corruption*. Oslo, Norway: United Nations Development Programme.

"Justice Minister, Aondoakaa, Divides Nigerians, As Confusion Ravages War On Corruption" (2007). *Vanguard*. September 21:19.

Kalu, Orji (2011). "Challenges before President Jonathan". *Saturday Sun*. May 7.

"Lamorde Shakes Up EFCC" (2012). *The Nation on Sunday*. March 11.

Lazarsfeld, P.F. and Allan Barton (1951). "Qualitative Measurement in the Social Sciences: Classification, Typologies and Indices", in Daniel Lerner and Harold D. Lasswell (eds.) *The Policy Science Recent Developments in Scope and Method*. New York: Stanford University Press.

Lazarsfeld, P.F. and Allan Barton (1961). "Some Functions of Qualitative Analysis in Sociological Research", in S.M. Lipset and Neil J. Smelser, *Sociology: The Progress of a Decade*. New Jersey: Prentice-Hall, Inc.

Leedy, P. (1989). *Practical Research: Planning and Design*. 4th edn. New York: Macmillan.

"Looting the loot" (2013:19). *The Nation*. July 24.

Maikano, D.I. (2013). "Of state pardon and Ribadu's frustrations". *The Nation*. March 12.

Marenin, Otwin (1982). "Policing African State: Toward a Critique." *Comparative Politics.* Vol. 14, No. 4. July (pages 379 – 396).

Merriam, S.B. (1988). *Case Study Research in Education: A Qualitative Approach.* San Francisco, CA: Jossey-Bass.

Miracle, A.W. (1981). "Cross-Cultural Research and The Role of Anthropology in Criminal Justice." *Journal of Criminal Justice: An International Journal.* Vol. 9 (pages 383 – 388).

"Much Ado About 419" (1992). *Daily Times.* February 27.

Munck, Gerado L. (2009). *Measuring Democracy: A Bridge Between Scholarship and Politics.* Baltimore, MD: John Hopkins University Press.

Murray, Rowena (2009). *How to Write a Thesis.* London: Open University Press.

"₦10 Billion Loan Controversy: Your action is in bad Faith" (2011). *Sunday Sun.* June 2.

Ndibe, Okey (2011). "Time For a New Anti-Corruption Manual". *Daily Sun.* June 7.

"Nigeria Arrests runaway Governor" (2005). BBC. December 9. (http://new.bbc.co.uk/2/Africa/ 4513172.stm).

"Nigeria: EFCC, ICPC Lack Capacity to Investigate (2011). *Daily Trust.* July 1.

"Nigeria Loses ₦1.26 Billion Revenue to Fraudsters" (1995). *The Guardian.* November 5.

"Nigeria Second Most Corrupt Nation" (2002). *Vanguard.* August 29.

"Nigeria's Application of Plea Bargain Decries" (2012). *Vanguard.* April 4.

"Nigerians Abroad" (1993). *National Concord.* October 27.

Nigerians Have Lost Faith in EFCC (2011) (elombahperspective@gmail.com).

"No Gov Cleared Yet – EFCC" (2006). *Vanguard.* October 10:1, 15.

"No Governor Cleared" (2006). *Vanguard.* October 10.

"No Plea Bargaining" (2012:19). *The Nation.* September 2.

"No Tears for Farida" (2011). *Tell.* December 5.

Nwosu, I. (2011). "The EFCC Shake-up". *Saturday Sun.* November 26.

Obi, A. (2011). "Farida Lost to the Brotherhood". *Daily Sun.* December 8.

Obijiofor, L. (2012:19). "EFCC As A Weakened Watchdog." *Daily Sun.* July 11.

Obijiofor, L. (2012:56). "A Hopeless EFCC and a Corrupt Judiciary" *Daily Sun.* November 28.

Ocheje, P.D. (2001). "Law & Social Change: Socio-Legal Analysis of Nigeria's Corrupt Practices & Other Related Offences Act, 2000". 445, *Journal of African Law.* 173.

Odusile, W. (2012:22). "EFCC: Same Old Story." *The Nation.* November 27.

Ofunwa Villager (2008). "Re: A Letter to Mrs. Farida Waziri, EFCC Chairman". *Posted:* July 29.

Ohia, Ike (2011). *Reaction.* June 15.

Ojinnaka, O. (2011). "US Solicits More Power for EFCC to Fight Crime". *Economic Crime.* January 13.

Ojo, Olasupo (undated). "Nigeria's EFCC Waning Anti-Corruption War". Committee for the Defense of Human Rights (CDHR).

Okoro, J. (2013:24). "EFCC, another arm of police". *Daily Sun.* August 5.

Okotie, Tosan (2008). "A Letter to Mrs. Farida Waziri, EFCC Chairman." *Posted:* Texas, USA: July 29.

Olabulo, O. and Y. Gbenga-Ogundare (2011). "Corruption: 26 ex-govs under investigation – EFCC. Says Judiciary gives succour to corrupt politicians." *Posted:* August 12, Lagos.

Olowo, A.O. (2010). "Nigeria: And The EFCC Goofed" *Comments.* October 28. Abuja, Nigeria.

Olumhense, S. (2008). "The Anatomy of Corruption." *Nigeria Village Square.* November 22.

Omatseye, S. (2012:64). "Whited Sepulchre." *The Nation.* May 14.

Omotunde, S. (2012:21). "Kleptocracy Unlimited: Why Nigeria Isn't Working." *The Nation*. May 7.

"On Corruption" (2002). Catholic Secretariat Forum. *The Guardian*. September 8.

Onyema, E. (undated). "EFCC and Plea Bargaining Issue in Nigeria: Matters Arising." *Crime Free and Peace Initiative*.

"Orji Kalu: Challenges Before President Jonathan" (2011). *Saturday Sun*. May 7:71.

Oromaner, M.J. (1968). "The Most Cited Sociologists." *The American Sociologist*. Vol. 3. May (pages 124 – 126).

Oromaner, M.J. (1969). "The Audience as a Determinant of the Most Important Sociologists." *The American Sociologist*. Vol. 4, November (pages 332 – 335).

Osagie, E. (2011). "Nigeria: The Coming Revolution". *Daily Sun*. June 20.

Oshunkeye, Shola (2013). "While I was away..." *Sunday Sun*. March 31.

"Our Stand on Plea Bargain – EFCC" (2011). *Tribune*. November 19.

Oyewo, Oyelowo (undated). "Constitutions, Governance and Corruption: Challenges and Prospects for Nigeria." Undated paper.

"Panel: Scrap EFCC, ICPC, FRSC, Others" (2012). *The Nation*. April 17.

"Persecution of Ex-Bank Directors" (2011). *Daily Sun*. May 23:20.

Philips, E.M. and D.S. (2000). *How to Get a Ph.D.: A Handbook For Students and Their Supervisors*. 3rd edn. Buckingham: Open University Press.

"Plea Bargain a tool to help the rich escape justice, says Mark" (2012). *The Nation*. April 3.

"Pocket Cartoon" (2012). *Vanguard*. April 4.

Pope, J. (2000). *TI Source Book: Confronting Corruption: The Elements of a National Integrity System*. Berlin: Transparency International.

Powell, C. (1995). "Abacha's CIA Record". *Tempo*. October 12.

"Presidential Jailbreak" (2013). *The Nation*. March 17.

"Removal of Waziri as EFCC Boss" (2011). *Daily Sun*. November 30.

Ribadu, N. (2006). "EFCC: Between Perception And Reality". *ThisDay*. May 31.

Ribadu, N. (2009). "Capital Loss and Corruption: The Example of Nigeria". Testimony Before The House Financial Services Committee (U.S.). May 10.

"Ribadu's Course" (2008). *The Nation*. January 7:13.

"Ribadu's Dismissal: A Blow Against Hope" (2009). *Tell*. January 12:20.

Ribadu, N. (2013:21). "Truths, lies and my EFCC days." *Daily Sun*. July 23.

Salami, A.T. (2007). "The EFCC of Nigeria: A Political Science Analysis." *Nigerian Forum*. Vol. 28, Nos 5 – 6. May-June.

"Senate Clears Lamorde" (2012). *The Nation*. February 16.

Shichor, D. (1982). "An Analysis of Citations in Introductory Criminology Textbook: A Research Note". *Journal of Criminal Justice: An International Journal*. Vol. 10 (pages 231 – 237).

Shuaib, Y.A. (2005). "Re: EFCC, Corruption And The Rest of Us". *The Punch*. January 12.

Sik, Endre (2002). "The Bad, the Worse & the Worst: Guesstimating the Level of Corruption" in *Political Corruption in Transition: A Skeptic's Handbook*, Stephen Kotkin and Andras Sajo (eds.) Budapest: Central University Press. (91-113).

"Special Courts for Corruption Cases" (2011). *Daily Sun*. November 8.

"The AG Means Well" (2009). *Tell*. September, 28.

"The Bankole Saga" (2011). *The Nation*. June 12.

"The Criteria for EFCC Leadership" (2012). *The Guardian*. March 22.

"The Fall of Farida" (2011). *The News*. December 5.

"The Game Plan" (2011). *The Guardian.* June 6.

"The New Anti-Crime Czar" (2003). *THISDAY*, August 30:45.

"The Plea Bargain Controversy" (2012). *Sunday Sun.* March 11.

"They Must Pay" (1995). London. *The Sunday Telegraph.* November 12.

Ugwuonye, E.E. (2011a). "Challenges Before Lamorde: Refocusing The War Against Corruption". http:// links.causes.com/s/blj/pe.

Ugwuonye, E.E. (2011b). "Discredited EFCC: Another Nigerian Disaster-Reports". *Republic Report.* New York. May 30.

Ugwuonye, E.E. (2011c). "EFCC and Nigeria Failed The Test; All Their Pretenses Were Shattered to Pieces and No Illusions, About It". *Republic Report*, New York, May 18.

Ugwuonye, E.E. (2011d). "EFCC: Farida Waziri's case beyond a Question of Competence" (http://elombah.com/index. php?August3).

Ugwuonye, Emeka (2011d). "EFCC: Another Nigerian Disaster". June 7.

"Undertaker Takes Over EFCC: Rest In Piece!" (2008). *Tell.* June 2.

US Applauds Jonathan on Waziri's removal" (2011). *Daily Sun.* December 9.

Utomi, P. (1995). "In Defence of Powell". *The Guardian*. October 9.

Uzondu, James (2010). "Between EFCC And 'Corrupt' Politicians". *Facebook Posted*: November 1.

Vukor-Quarshie, G.M.K. (1996). "Development in the Criminal Law of Nigeria: Economic & Business Crimes". *Nigerian Current Law Review*.

"Waziri Wants Tough Measures to Fight Corruption" (2011). *The Nation*. May 6:6.

Waziri, F. (2011a). Untitled paper presented at the United Nations Conference On Least Developed Countries (LDV – IV), Istanbul, Turkey.

Waziri, F. (2011b). "The Economic and Financial Crimes Commission's (EFCC's) Critical Role in Growing The Economy." Paper presented to the Nigeria-British Chamber of Commerce, Monday May 16.

"What are the roles of ICPC and EFCC in Nigeria". (2010). *Posted:* November 5.

"What is your view on plea bargaining of Ex-Governors with EFCC" (2007). *Vanguard*. August 10.

"What Nigerians Expect From Jonathan" (2011). *Sunday Sun*. May 8:64.

"Why EFCC is in a Comma" (2008). *Tell*. 48 December 1.

"Why Encourage Plea Bargaining in Nigeria" (2012:15). *The Nation*. September 2.

"Why Farida Waziri was fired" (2011). *Daily Sun*. November 24.

"Yar'Adua Ends Anti-Corruption War" (2008). *Tell*. No. 2, January.

Index

1999 Constitution, 166, 171
1999 Nigerian Constitution, 26
Abbas, 161
Abdul Suleiman, 103
Abdullahi Adamu, 149
Adebayo Alao-Akala, 176
Adeniyi, 76
Adeoye and Ezeamalu, 2011, 145
Advance Fee Fraud and Other
    Related Offences Act, 1995, 52
Advance Fee Fraud, 63, 66, 144
African Development Bank, 162
Ahmad Abdurrahmah, 103
Akaridi, 35
Akhikhero, 14
Algeria, 30
Aliyu Akwe Doma, 149, 176
Amount of Money Allegedly
    Misappropriated in Federal
    Government Ministries, 40
Anderson *et al.*, 5
Angola, 37
Anti-corruption Revolution
    Campaign (ANCOR)., 67, 176
Anti-corruption Transparency
    Committee (ACTC), 101
Aondoakaa, 12, 13, 68, 71, 75
Armenia, 30
Asemota, 35
Audu, 11
Ayo Olowonihi, 105

Ayobolu, 114
Azerbaijan, 30, 37

Babafemi, 123, 129
Babalola Aborishade, 68, 176
Bain, 28
Bala Sanga, 105
Bangladesh, 34, 37
Bank Fraud in Nigeria From 1989 to
    1999, 38
Banks and Other Financial
    Institutions Act, 1991, 54, 142
Bello Imam, 15, 16, 17, 18, 59, 64
Bode George, 68, 176
Bola Ajibola, 12, 123
Boni Haruna, 176
Borg and Gall, 8, 19, 130
Bosnia-Herzegovina, 30
Brazil, 30
Brew, 31
British Broadcasting Corporation
    (BBC), 44
Bruce, 6, 7, 8, 21

Cameroon, 33, 37
Cecilia Ibru, 115, 146, 160
Central Intelligence Agency (CIA),
    110, 111
Chimaroke Nnamani, 149
China, 30
Coca-Cola, 178

Code of Conduct Commission (CCC)., 99
Code of Conduct Commission, 1, 2
Code of Conduct Tribunal, 100
Collin Powell, 34
Columbia, 30
Composition of the Commission, 47
Conference of Nigerian Political Parties (CNPP), 77
Contextual relevance of EFCC, 13
Cooper, 7
Corrupt Practices and Other Related Offences Act 2000, 26
Cyber crimes, 67

Dahiru Musdapher, 125
Danjuma Goje, 176
Dare, 90
Dariye, 11
David Mark, 126
Deborah Maclean, 106
Defence Intelligence Agency (DIA), 1, 111
Diepreye S.P.Alamieyeseigha, 117, 149
Dimeji Bankole, 24, 68, 77, 78, 80, 176
David Tukura, 105
Duncan, 29

Economic and Financial Crimes Commission (EFCC), 1-4, 9-32, 36, 40-42, 44, 45, 46, 57, 58, 59, 61-76, 78-93, 95-114, 118, 121-137, 139-157, 159, 142-147, 161, 162
EFCC (Establishment Act) 2004, 9, 26
EFCC Appraisal Indices, 133
EFCC *Handbook*, 42

EFCC Performance Appraisal Mandate-Specific Scorecard, 139
EFCC Review Boards, 170
EFCC Under President Goodluck Jonathan, 76, 79
EFCC Under President Olusegun Obasanjo, 71, 79
EFCC Under President Umaru Yar'adua, 74
Elombah EFCC Report, 161
El-Rufai, 68
Emine, 147
Enweremadu, 16, 18, 73
Erastus Akingbola, 14, 176
Ethno-Religious Domination of Top and Strategic Positions, 103
Evil geniuses, 34
Eya, 85, 87

Failed Banks (Recovery of Debt and Financial Malpractices in Banks) Act, 54
Faridi Waziri, 14, 18, 20, 21, 26, 42, 61, 65, 67, 68, 74, 77, 78, 79, 82, 83, 85, 88, 89, 90-92, 99, 114, 128, 135, 144, 147-149, 155
Federal Bureau of Intelligence (FBI), 63, 110, 111
Federal Civil Service Commission, 113
Federal Inland Revenue Service, 60, 63
Federal Road Safety Commission (FRSC), 102
Femi Fani-Kayode, 68, 176
Financial Action Task Force, 45
Financial Crimes Commission (Establishment, etc.) Act 2004, 45
Financial Malpractices in Bank Act 2004, 27

Findings on EFCC, 139, 140
Forgery and Fraud Cases in Nigerian
  Banks, 39
Francis Atuche, 160
Freedom of Information Bill, 169
Friedrich Ebert Stiftung Foundation,,
  18

Gabriel, 145
Gary Henry, 24
Gbenga Daniel, 176
Georgia, 30
Ghana, 30
Global Integrity Report, 30
Global Integrity, 28, 29, 30
GoAML, 177
GoCase, 177
Goodluck Jonathan regime, 81
Google, 178
Government interference, 141

Haruna, 79
Hassan Lawal, 176
Henry Kissinger, 111
Hillary Clinton, 97
Historical background, legal status
  and organisational structure of the
  EFCC, 33
History and rationale for the
  establishment of the EFCC, 40
Human Rights Watch, 149

Ibrahim Adoke, 103
Ibrahim Lamorde, 81, 82, 90, 103
  105
Independent Corrupt Practices and
  Other Related Offences Commission
  (ICPC), 1, 3, 4, 41, 44, 73, 91,
  95, 96,100, 101, 105, 106, 135,
  146, 157, 164, 165

India, 30
Indonesia, 30, 37
International Labour Organisation
  (ILO) Conference, 92
Interpretation, 5, 6
Iyabo Obasanjo-Bello, 68

James Ibori, 12, 76
Jerryboy, 18
Johnnie Carson, 82
Joshua Dariye, 149

Kenny Martins, 68
Kenya, 37

Lamorde, 90, 105, 138
Leadership immaturity and
  garrulousity, 155
Lebanon, 30
Leedy, 6, 8
Legal status and organizational
  structure of the, 45
Lucky Igbinedion, 12

M.K.O Abiola, 79
Macedonia, 30
Madagascar, 37
Malawi, 30
Menace of economic and financial
  crimes, 153
Merriam, 5, 6, 8, 19
Mexico, 30
Michael Botmang, 176
Microsoft, 178
Millennium Challenge Corporation,
  30
Miscellaneous Offences Act (Cap.
  410 LFN), 54, 144
Mobolaji Sanusi, 80
Mohammed Wakili, 105

Moldova, 37
Money Laundering (Amendment Act) 2004, 26, 54
Money Laundering Amendment Act 2003, 144
Mongolia, 30
Most Corrupt Three Nations in the World, 37
Mustapha, 14, 16

Namadi Sambo, 177
Nasir El-Rufai, 176
National Agency For Food and Drug Administration and Control, 1
National Copyright Commission, 1
National Drug Law Enforcement Agency, 1
National Intelligence Agency (NIA), 1, 111
Ndibe, 77, 160
Nepal, 30
Nicaragua, 30
Niger Delta Region, 64
Nigeria Customs Service, 64
Nigeria Police Force (NPF), 1, 2, 105
Nigeria Security and Civil Defence Corps (NSCD), 105
Nigerian Catholic Secretariat Forum, 35
Norway, 30
National Security Agency (NSA), 110, 111
Nuhu Ribadu, 62, 63, 64, 81, 98, 99, 108, 109, 159
Nwosu, 95

Obasanjo and Yar'Adua, 18
Obi, 98, 99
Ocheje, 14
Ojo, 157

Olaolu Adegbite, 105
Olusegun Obasanjo government, 36
Ombudsman, 155
Onyema, 114, 125
Orji Kalu, 11, 12, 71, 83
Oromaner, 27
Oronsaye, 106
Osita Nwajah, 105

Paraguay, 37
Performance of the EFCC, 61, 62, 71, 74, 76, 85, 93, 107, 130, 132, 133, 134, 143
Phillips and Pugh, 8
Plea bargain with the agency, 116
Plea Bargain, 116, 117, 118, 120, 121, 126, 127, 129
Politically Exposed Persons (PEPs) Standing Trial Who Contested During the 2007 and 2011 Polls, 70
President George Bush, 65
President Goodluck Jonathan, 76, 79, 97
President Olusegun Obasanjo, 18, 36, 41, 42, 44, 65, 69, 71, 73, 91, 146
President Umaru Yar'Adua, 11, 12, 18, 24, 74, 75, 76, 85
Presidential Committee on the Rationalization and Restructuring of Federal Government Parastatals, Commissions and Agencies, 105
Project Eagle Claw, 176
Purpose, 5, 6, 7, 8

Qatar, 30

Rabiu Muazu, 103
Ranking of Functional Performance of EFCC, 144

Rasheed Ladoja, 176
Rationale for writing the literature review, 6
Rationale, benefits and challenges, 27
Recommendations, 153, 163
Recoveries from June 2008 to March 2011, 69
Related Investigations and Convictions from 2003 to 2011, 69
Review of Relevant Literature, 5
Ribadu, 11, 16, 17, 18, 36, 37, 59, 62, 71, 72, 84, 85, 89, 94, 144, 146, 147, 148, 158
Rwanda, 30

Salami, 17, 18, 44, 105, 136
Sam Egwu, 149
Saminu Turaki, 149
Sebastian Adigwe, 176
Serbia, 30
Shichor, 27
Sierra Leone, 30
Slovakia, 30
Source and method of data collection, 23
South Korea,, 30
Special Financial and Economic Crimes Courts, 165
Special powers of the Commission, 53
State Security Service (SSS), 1, 111
Steve Oronsaye, 105
Synthesis, 5, 6, 7, 19
Syria, 30

Tafa Balogun, 108, 117, 149
Ten Most Corrupt Nations in the World, 37
Terence McCulley, 97
The Failed Banks (Recovery of Debts) and Financial Malpractices in Banks Act 1994, 26, 144
The Global Integrity Report, 29
The Miscellaneous Offences Act, 26
The research setting, 21
Thomas L. Friedman, 35
Training and Research Institute, TRI, 178
Transactions Clearing Platform (TCP), 176
Transparency International (TI), 33-35, 37, 38, 41, 63, 80
Transparency Nigeria, 25
Trinidad, 30
Turaki, 11
Turkey, 65, 69

U.S. Postal Service, 63
Uganda, 30
Ugwuonye, 103, 167
Ukraine, 30
United Arab Emirate, 30
United Nations Conference on Least Developed Countries, 18, 65
United Nations, 41, 147
United States, 30
USAID, 29

Venezuela, 30
Vietnam, 30
Vukor-Quarshie, 14

West African Summit, 178
Western Union, 178
Wikileaks, 24
World Bank, 29

Yahoo!, 178

Zbigniew Brzezinski, 109
Zimbabwe, 30

www.ingramcontent.com/pod-product-compliance
Lightning Source LLC
Chambersburg PA
CBHW060035030426
42334CB00019B/2332